Building a Home

IN A PULL-APART WORLD

**Powerful principles
for a happier marriage:
*4 steps that work***

Bill & Vonette Bright

NewLife
PUBLICATIONS
A MINISTRY OF CAMPUS CRUSADE FOR CHRIST

Building a Home in a Pull-Apart World

Published by
New*Life* Publications
A ministry of Campus Crusade for Christ
100 Sunport Lane
Orlando, FL 32809

Design and typesetting by Genesis Publications.

Printed in the United States of America.

Library of Congress Cataloging-in-Publication Data
Bright, Bill.
    Building a home in a pull-apart world : powerful principles for a happier marriage : four steps that work / Bill and Vonette Bright.
        p.   cm.
    Includes bibliographical references.
    ISBN 1-56399-058-X
    1. Marriage—Religious aspects—Christianity. 2. Family—Religious life. I. Bright, Vonette Z.   II. Title.
    BV835.B68   1995
    248.8'44—dc20   94-45053
                                                                          CIP

Unless otherwise indicated, Scripture quotations are taken from the *New American Standard Bible*, ©1960, 1962, 1963, 1968, 1971, 1972, 1975, 1977 by the Lockman Foundation, La Habra, California.
Scripture quotations designated TLB are from *The Living Bible*, ©1971 by Tyndale House Publishers, Wheaton, Illinois.
Scripture quotations designated RSV are from the *Revised Standard Version*, ©1952 by Thomas Nelson & Sons, New York.
Scripture quotations designated NKJ are from the *New King James* version, ©1979, 1980, 1982 by Thomas Nelson Inc., Publishers, Nashville, Tennessee.
Scripture quotations designated NIV are from the *New International Version*, ©1973, 1978, 1984 by the International Bible Society. Published by Zondervan Bible Publishers, Grand Rapids, Michigan.

For more information, write:
L.I.F.E.—P. O. Box 40, Flemmington Markets, 2129, Australia
Campus Crusade for Christ of Canada—Box 300, Vancouver, B.C., V6C 2X3, Canada
Campus Crusade for Christ—Fairgate House, King's Road, Tyseley, Birmingham, B11 2AA, England
Lay Institute for Evangelism—P. O. Box 8786, Auckland 3, New Zealand
Campus Crusade for Christ—Alexandra, P. O. Box 0205, Singapore 9115, Singapore
Great Commission Movement of Nigeria—P. O. Box 500, Jos, Plateau State Nigeria, West Africa
Campus Crusade for Christ International—100 Sunport Lane, Orlando, FL 32809, USA

As a personal policy, Bill and Vonette Bright have never accepted honorariums or royalties for their personal use. Any royalties from this book or the many other books by Bill Bright are dedicated to the glory of God and designated to the various ministries of Campus Crusade for Christ/*NewLife2000*.

"A 'Must-Read' Book"

"A candid peek into the lives of two effective and faithful Christian leaders who made their ministry and marriage work. In these pages you will not find an aloof relationship that you're unable to relate to, but an honest look at two people who can help you deal with the pressures in *your* day-to-day life. This is a 'must read' book!"

Dennis Rainey
Director, FamilyLife

"There are no hairline cracks in this marriage. Bill and Vonette Bright love each other in a manner that not even their fast pace as two world travelers can shake. We highly recommend this book, written by two close friends and role models."

Howard and Jeanne Hendricks
Chairman, Center for Christian Leadership
Distinguished Professor, Dallas Theological
Seminary

"Bill's and Vonette's new book is a wonderful example of how a traditional marriage can work. Their marriage illustrates many refreshing, unexpected, important ideas in building a stronger marriage. The practice of other-centered living described in this book is a beautiful testimony of what God can do with a man and a woman determined to love each other as Jesus Christ loved us."

Lyle Larson, Ph.D.
Department of Sociology
University of Alberta

"*Building a Home* is solidly biblical, delightfully readable, and eminently practical."

Norman Archer
International Bible Teacher
Victoria, British Columbia

"Even to those of us who have a good marriage, this book will reinforce God's principles for daily living. For those who are going through turbulence in their marriage, Bill and Vonette have obviously worked out a practical guide for a Christ-centered happy union and home."

Betty Thiessen
Co-host, "It's a New Day"
Winnipeg, Manitoba

"Bill and Vonette Bright uncover some unique treasures to secure and bless God's beautiful gift of the family. Here is a book on the family that draws from the richest resource in the world—God's Word. And mined from one of life's greatest teachers—experience."

Ravi Zacharias
Ravi Zacharias International Ministries

"*Building a Home in a Pull-Apart World* is a breath of fresh air. For years I've wanted to hear Bill and Vonette share their insights on a marriage that has been a model for Dottie and me—and now we have the tremendous benefits of their lives together."

Josh McDowell
Josh McDowell Ministry

"Those who read *Building a Home in a Pull-Apart World* will discover practical, biblical principles for developing an intimate and fulfilling marriage."

Dr. Ron Mayforth
Senior Pastor, Central Baptist Church
Edmonton, Alberta

"A real-life look at a marriage that works."

Lynne A. Smith
Speaker and Bible Teacher, Women Alive
Edmonton, Alberta

Contents

ॐ

To our beloved sons Zac and Brad and our daughters-in-love Terry and Katherine. And to all of the many staff members of Campus Crusade for Christ who through the years have served the Lord as our personal associates. You have helped to maximize our daily schedules, enabling us to have a more active and fruitful ministry, both individually and together. You know us so well and have helped to make us what we are. We trust you are pleased with the product you helped produce. You are dearly loved and greatly appreciated.

Acknowledgments

WELL, WORLD, here it is—almost fifty years of joyful, adventuresome life together, expressed in words and story revealing the principles that have kept our marriage vibrant, exciting, and alive. We have endeavored to be honest, frank, and practical to help you—as a couple, or as a single person contemplating marriage—to live a full and rewarding life as you seek to build your home in this pull-apart world.

Vonette and I are deeply grateful to God for giving us the opportunity to be involved together in a worldwide ministry for our dear Lord. The Holy Spirit has provided the glue that keeps us together. And God alone deserves the honor and glory for our accomplishments.

Many have contributed to our growing insights and helped enrich our relationship with each other, but we are especially aware of the contributions made by the staff of Campus Crusade for Christ. Apart from our family, they are the most important people in the world to us. They help make so much of what we do possible. Many of our most exciting moments as a couple have been with our beloved staff.

This book has been a team effort involving writers and researchers Don Tanner, Joette Whims, Jean Bryant, and Barbara Fagan. They spent many hours with the manuscript, helping us to articulate what God has taught us about the joy of biblical marriage, making commitments to

God and each other, and living each day in His presence
and for His glory.

Special thanks to our associates for reading the manuscript and providing most helpful comments: Steve
Douglass, executive vice president of Campus Crusade for
Christ; Judy Douglass, former editor of *Worldwide Challenge*; Dennis Rainey, director of FamilyLife; Mary Graham, director of radio for Women Today; and Steve Sellers,
national director of the Campus Ministry.

We are also deeply grateful for the valued comments of
those who have given their endorsements of this book, in
both the United States and Canada.

Thank you, all who have labored with us to make this
book a reality. To God be the glory!

Chapter 1

The Uninvited Guest

&

L ADIES AND gentlemen, please remain in your seats and keep your seat belts fastened. We should be out of this in a few moments..."

The calm voice over the intercom was hardly reassuring as our Pan Am 707 pierced the fury of a storm during our flight from New York to Washington, D.C. The sky flashed with lightning's forked tongue, seemingly just inches away from the plane. Swirling winds tore at the plane's metal skin, and the aircraft bounced and shuddered in the turbulence.

Vonette and Dr. David Hock Tey, director of Chinese Ministries for Campus Crusade for Christ, sat on each side of me, and our son Brad had settled into the seat directly across the aisle.

I gripped Vonette's hand and turned to look at her strained face, letting my eyes drink in every beloved curve.

"I don't know how much longer the plane can endure this storm without breaking into pieces," I worried.

She nodded gravely.

Leaning over Vonette to peer out the window, I saw almost continuous lightning streak across the sky. With each threatening bolt, the sky seemed to explode in brilliant flashes. We appeared to be in the heart of a ball of white fire.

The 707 began to twist—first to the right, then to the left—in the increasing fury. The shaky laughter around me faded into an eerie silence, broken only by the calm voice of the flight attendant. Through the windows we could see the wings flapping almost like those of a giant bird struggling frantically against a violent downdraft.

Beside me, David began rocking and chanting in his Oriental fashion, "O God. O Lord, save us. O God, O Lord, save us."

Vonette leaned toward me, and I felt the gentle pressure of her hand entwined in mine. Softly, we began praying, our words flowing together in supplication to our precious Savior.

Convinced that our aircraft could not survive the turbulence much longer, I tenderly said goodbye to my dear Vonette and she to me. Then, together, we told our wonderful Lord that we were ready to come to Him if He desired.

Immediately, we sensed a peace flowing over us like a gentle river, a stillness that quieted our fears as though we had just nestled into a serene cocoon. Vonette's hand relaxed in mine, and we leaned over David to reassure Brad. He had heard us saying our goodbyes.

"We love you, Son," I said solemnly. Vonette echoed my statement with a mother's compassionate gaze.

He smiled wanly, his face ashen.

The prayers and consolations of our little group were the only sounds coming from the cabin. Suddenly, I thought of how the Lord Jesus had calmed the winds and water on the sea when His disciples feared that their boat would capsize during another violent storm. Knowing His power and love for all of His children, I prayed aloud, "Lord, You are the God of all creation. You control the laws of nature. You quieted the storm on the Sea of Galilee. We ask You to quiet this storm!"

Immediately the rain and the turbulence stopped.

Vonette stared at me in amazement, then smiled slightly. "Now, why didn't we pray that prayer earlier?"

I squeezed her hand and grinned back. Our fragile plane flew on, threading through the thick darkness abandoned by the lightning. You can be sure that Vonette and I continued to thank and praise the Lord for hearing our prayers and saving our lives. Hours later, the pilot skillfully brought the plane down in a smooth landing at a freight terminal in Norfolk, a long way from our destination. The flight that should have lasted sixty-five minutes had become a four-hour nightmare of blind flying and had taken us to a small airport in Virginia.

We learned later that the lightning had knocked a huge hole in the fuselage near the cockpit, destroying all the radar equipment. The pilot said this was the most violent storm he had ever experienced in many millions of miles of flying.

Vonette and I did make it on time to our meetings in Washington the next morning, thanks to an all-night bus. We have experienced many other stresses since our marriage on December 30, 1948, but few have been as dramatic as that one.

Some marriages, I have observed, closely resemble that stormy flight, although others seem like the quiet waters of a lake at sunrise.

The media and some Christians would like us to believe that all marriages should be like the quiet lake. Thus when a couple's relationship becomes violently stormy, many spouses feel it is simply too tough to handle; the external and internal stresses are more than they can bear, and they opt out of the marriage.

Stress Comes Unexpectedly

Stress in marriage often comes unexpectedly—like an uninvited guest who suddenly appears at your door when you least expect him.

Have you ever opened the door to someone from out of town who was completely unexpected? Did you feel invaded? Whether the uninvited guest is a relative, a friend, or the friend of a friend, he can force us into special efforts because we did not expect him, nor were we mentally or emotionally prepared for his visit. It interrupts our planned activity, and it can even create relationship problems in our home.

Imagine now that this guest at your door pushes past you without waiting for you to ask him in. He plops down on your couch and makes himself comfortable, indicating that he is there to stay. It appears to you that he will be here for weeks, maybe months, and you realize that you may just have to learn to cope with him. You begin to identify his habits and try to get to know him well enough that you can adapt your lifestyle comfortably to his commands.

In an attempt to predict his moves, you try to memorize his face, noting every line and analyzing all his expressions. But just about the time you think you have it mastered, one morning he walks pompously into the breakfast room and sits down, looking at you with a totally different face. Dismayed, you realize that your guest had been wearing a mask. So you now begin to study this new face. Yet, before you figure it out, he changes faces again.

No matter how quickly you discern what's behind each new face, you can't keep up with him because he keeps switching. His persistent ever-changing presence keeps both you and your entire family in a state of turmoil as you continually try to adjust.

Who is this ill-mannered, unwanted guest?

Vonette and I have seen the many faces of this uninvited guest, and we have learned to recognize him as "stress." He particularly personifies the dual pressures of a career and a fast-paced lifestyle.

The unexpectedness of the presence of stress is one of the key factors affecting our response to it. After all, we think, stress may be common in the marriage where one or both partners are nonbelievers, but for Christians? If Christ is resident in us and we are filled with the Holy Spirit, should we experience stress?

Yes, unfortunately, stress can come to even the most dedicated Christian couples, and it usually is a surprise when we realize what is happening. We may try to prepare for it, but no matter how much we do, it still catches us off-guard.

Excessive Stress

All marriages experience varied patterns and degrees of stress that, if not attended to when we become aware of them, can wreck the marriage and destroy the home. We know well how a busy lifestyle adds extraordinary pressure to a relationship.

These factors, all related to stress, are intricately involved as we attempt to build a home in a pull-apart world.

Stress comes unbidden; stress moves in relentlessly; stress is difficult to understand or predict. The changing faces of excessive stress take an enormous emotional toll, which sometimes results in frightening physical reactions. Stress stimulates our adrenal glands to produce the adrenaline we need for "fight or flight." When we are not allowed to burn those secretions, as is usually the case in our modern world, we suffer physically. We all have heard about illnesses and accidents presumably brought about because the victims were under severe stress. Violent arguments, abuse, separation, and divorce are also among the tragic results of people being under extreme pressure.

Although some stress is essential in healthy survival, we recognize that too much is potentially dangerous to our health, our relationships, and our families. In considering how stress affects couples who are attempting to build a stable home in today's pull-apart world, we realize that we must learn to recognize the uninvited guest and take steps to discourage him.

Is excessive stress an unavoidable part of our lives? Do we have to let the uninvited guest disturb the tranquility of our homes? Definitely not. We choose the amount of stress we will feel by deciding how we will respond to its causes.

In spite of the divorce statistics, and the many stresses that work against us, I remain optimistic about the value and the durability of marriage. I believe we can develop response patterns that will deepen the intimacy in our relationships and enable us to build godly homes despite the pressures of our world pulling us apart.

Looking Ahead

Years ago, my dearly beloved pastor, Dr. Louis Evans, Sr., used to say, "Marriage is God's idea and only with His help can we work it out with joy."

In the coming pages we will show you how to build your home with the guidance and power of the Holy Spirit. We will share four vital steps for building a home in this world no matter how the world pulls us apart, and we will show you how applying these principles will help you build stronger relationships with the Lord and with your mate.

Our Lord has not promised us a stress-free life. We find that some of the greatest heroes of the Bible lived under extremely harsh circumstances. For example, David watched two of his sons rebel against his leadership; Joseph was unjustly accused of attacking Potiphar's wife; and the apostle Paul endured beatings and imprisonment. Yet in all of their difficulties, these and other faithful men and women triumphed through the enabling power of the Holy Spirit.

Applying these principles will help you build stronger relationships with the Lord and with your mate.

As Christians, we have an eternal advantage over the world. We can change the way we respond to both good and bad situations through the power of the Holy Spirit. Vonette and I want to share with you four secrets we have discovered that will help you experience victory over all of

your stresses and live a full and joyful life with your mate.
We invite you to see, as we have, that the Lord is faithful
even during the most stressful situations imaginable.

And do we have a few of those in case you'd like to
compare notes!

Vonette and I discovered that when you put a "vision-
ary" in a marriage with a "let's get things done" person,
that's a recipe for stress on a grand scale...

Step 1

Enter Into a Partnership

❧

God established marriage as a partnership.
But couples must consciously commit
themselves to the Lord and to each
other, and remain alert to any threat
to their union.

Chapter 2

Step 1: Enter Into a Partnership

ॐ

ALTHOUGH GOD ultimately holds the husband accountable for the leadership in the home, Vonette and I strongly believe that marriage is a partnership between equal participants. We believe the biblical truth that we are to become one (Genesis 2:24), and we try to model this in our relationship. But it hasn't been easy. Vonette clearly remembers the following incident:

Vonette
At one time, my changing role in the ministry put a serious strain on our relationship.

The move to Arrowhead Springs, California, in 1962 placed unusual demands on Bill. A man on our staff who didn't believe women should have a voice in business matters influenced him in certain decisions, and my counsel was no longer sought. That became a threat to our close partnership.

I should have talked it out with Bill when I began to feel hurt, but I didn't. He made decision after decision without me, and I felt left out. Often I heard about the changes long after they had been put into effect.

The situation finally came to a head when Bill and his administrator decided to place a print shop in the storage area of the hotel kitchen. They had taken over my area without a word to me. At the time, I was directing the kitchen and dining operations. I oversaw the purchase of food, and planned the meals for our many conferences. To do what they planned, they would have to cut into the kitchen vault where we kept our china, silver, and other valuable items.

Even though we weren't then using all the kitchen and storage space, we would need it eventually. And I didn't want to end up working in cramped quarters.

One Sunday morning, while Bill and I were dressing for church, he casually mentioned that decision.

I objected. Emphatically.

"Well, the decision has been made and it's too late to change our plans now," he asserted.

I saw the determination in his eyes and heard it in his voice. Suddenly, all the resentment that had been building inside me erupted. "Okay, Bill Bright! I'll just leave! I'm not going to live where I have nothing to say about what goes on."

Neither of us said anything more just then. I grabbed a few items of clothing for the children and myself and marched the boys to the car.

"Okay," Bill finally said, to my disappearing back, "if you feel so strongly, go on!"

I whisked the children into the car, got into the driver's seat and slumped down. I had no idea where to go. Tears welled up in my eyes. What would I do?

Zac, our nine-year-old, quickly cut to the core. "Mother, this shows me just what kind of person you really are."

His words stung, and I shook my head. *This is so stupid, leaving like this.* But Bill hadn't begged me to come back, and my pride wouldn't let me back down. I didn't want to leave Bill, but I didn't want to continue in a relationship where there was no regard for my opinion. My mind raced, trying to decide where to go.

Suddenly, Bill burst through the front door and strode to the front of the car. I would have to run over him to drive away. "Don't go, Vonette," he pleaded loudly. He looked pathetic, and I felt ashamed.

I don't remember any other words but those. I had acted foolishly, but wasn't ready to admit it and give in. "I won't be treated like a woman who has no contribution to make," I fumed.

Bill apologized; then I did too. I stayed because he took the first step toward reconciliation and working out our problems. It took a real man of God to admit he was wrong, and this gave me the courage to confess my poor attitude.

Bill promised he would find another place to put the print shop, but as it turned out, we had no other option. I began to realize that the real issue wasn't the location of the print shop. It was my expectation. I had counted on Bill to include me in his decision-making, but he unconsciously had diminished my part in the ministry. The lack of communication between us had seriously threatened our marriage.

This crisis showed us how vital our partnership was, and it helped us become more aware of how we must work at strengthening our relationship.

Bill

To establish partnership in marriage, couples must consciously commit themselves to the Lord and to each other, and they must remain alert to any threat to their union. This is the first step in building a godly home in a pull-apart world.

I really believe this commitment begins with the attitude of the husband. When he truly understands the importance of loving his wife as Christ loved the church (Ephesians 5:25), he will not demand to be served by his wife. Instead, he will ask himself, "How can I help her be God's maximum person? How can I help her enjoy life more and live less stressfully?"

Many of the counseling problems I encounter have started when the man insisted on his rights. And that attitude often prevails in Christian homes.

Building Your Partnership

God intended marriage to be the closest human bond. All too often, however, the stressors that invade a marriage pull spouses apart. We suggest three things you can do to build and strengthen your partnership and help protect it from these pressures.

First, *surrender your marriage to God.* To grow together, you and your spouse must yield yourselves fully to the Lord. This includes taking time to pray and discuss the scriptures together. With this spiritual foundation, your lives will begin to blend. You will learn to cope with the difficulties in your relationship—the irritations, frustrations, and differences between you.

Graciously, lovingly, encourage your mate to take an active role in your spiritual partnership. God understands you and your mate perfectly and can empower you with His Holy Spirit to build your spiritual relationship.

Second, *agree to walk together.* Early in our relationship, Vonette and I agreed that our partnership would not be my way or Vonette's way, but *our* way—serving the Lord together.

When a couple agree to walk together, they accept each other's beliefs, hopes, and desires, and they work through the expectations each brings to the relationship. This is a life-long process. Vonette and I are still discovering ways to improve our walk.

> *We agreed that our partnership would not be my way or Vonette's way, but our way—serving the Lord together.*
>
> ❧

Because we believe in this concept so much, Vonette and I insist that our Campus Crusade staff couples serve equally. Unless they have children, both partners are expected to be on the job. Neither spouse can work at another full- or part-time job, unless he or she is a volunteer.

The third thing you as a couple can do to protect your relationship is *share your dreams.* Sharing each other's dreams is vital to a partnership. Vonette and I have had many dreams through the years, but the single most important objective of our lives is to help fulfill the Great Commission of our Lord, as described in Matthew 28:19,20. This is our expression of our love for the

Lord, our deep gratitude for all that He has done for us, and our desire to obey Him.

Shortly after we totally surrendered our lives to each other and to our Lord, God gave me the vision for Campus Crusade for Christ. Signing our contract helped prepare our hearts to share the vision.

Vonette

Bill awakened me early one morning, hardly able to contain himself. He was bubbling over with enthusiasm and joy. Groggily, I sat up in bed and mumbled, "Let me get up, and I'll fix your breakfast."

"Honey, I don't need any breakfast." His intense enthusiasm overcame my desire to sink back into the pillows. Bill bustled out of the room. Springing out of bed, I slipped my robe from a hanger.

I found him standing in the living room pacing the floor. He was exuberant with laughter, tears rolling down his cheeks.

He spoke slowly without looking at me. His voice quivered.

"I now know what God wants us to do. Last night while I was studying, God spoke to me. Never have I felt His presence like that before! It happened so quickly. It was as if a huge canvas of the world were spread before me. Like an artist's hand sketching a sky, mountains, streams, and brooks, the painting showed only the high points, not the details. The Lord has shown me a broad plan for helping to take the gospel to the whole world.

"God has called me...God has called *us*, and He wants us to start by reaching students on the college campus."

At that time, Bill was operating his own fancy foods business and attending Fuller Theological Seminary. He had stayed up until midnight preparing for a Greek exam when suddenly God began speaking to him.

Pulling out a chair now, Bill sat down. His open textbooks lay on his desk. Closing the top one, he declared, "I'm dropping out of school. What God has told me to do is far more important than my final months of seminary."

Everything he had shared to this point was beautiful, but now he seemed to be overreacting. Imagine throwing away five years of study at Princeton and Fuller seminaries with all the credentials that soon would be in his hands!

"Honey, I can relate to students and laymen better as a layperson and business leader than as an ordained pastor," he insisted. "We're going to live by faith, Vonette. I want to sell the businesses and trade in that convertible for something modest. And we're going to have to move closer to the campus."

Bill's dream seemed too big for me, but I knew better than to say anything while he was so impassioned. Walking back into the bedroom, I felt the weight of such a radical change.

I was not ready to give up the financial security that Bill had provided. My mind raced. *I'm not the right wife for Bill. I could never accept the sacrifice.* I wanted a baby, and bottles of milk in the refrigerator, not just a cold formula of faith.

One afternoon, after several days of trying to convince Bill of other alternatives of combining business and ministry, I sank to my knees and buried my face in our white Martha Washington bedspread. "Oh, Lord," I cried, "if Bill is right, and this is right, I pray that You will give me a heart to respond."

I truly wanted to share Bill's dream. But I felt that the changes and sacrifices his new life would demand would bring far more pressure than I could handle. I had a college degree and was teaching a course of study I had written in the Los Angeles city schools. Eleanor Kalamus, who wrote a weekly syndicated newspaper column called "Glorify Yourself," was extracting chapters from my course for her column in the Hearst newspaper chain. Mrs. Kalamus was eager for my manuscript to be published, since in response to the column they already had 8,000 orders for my yet-to-be-completed book.

Would I have to abandon everything I wanted to do to follow Bill? Should I accept his vision and become his partner? I was of two minds. I wanted Bill to acknowledge my career potential, but at the same time I didn't want him to develop his ministry without me.

Bill's loving assurances and warmth made my struggle easier.

I realized I would never be happy outside his dream, and as he described his strategy for evangelism, I sensed an invisible altar waiting for me somewhere ahead. Gradually, the Lord Jesus drew me toward it and answered my prayer for a "heart to respond." I willingly put my sacrifices on that altar—my master's degree, my career, my book manuscript. Bill's dream had become my dream.

Not only has my life been richer, but just like Abraham when he offered up Isaac, the Lord has multiplied everything I gave up many times over. And He has enabled me to see and experience more than I ever could have done alone.

Bill

Sharing our dreams has given Vonette and me a sense of oneness. Although most couples do not have opportunities to work together as we do, all can choose a dream worthy of their united effort. Ask the Holy Spirit to help you catch the vision of partnership and experience oneness. Let your dreams draw you and your spouse together.

Make sure your visions are worthy of the calling the Lord has given you. Whether your dreams are simple and down-to-earth or grandiose and complicated, embrace your mate's aspirations with a sense of encouragement and excitement. As you share each other's dreams, you will experience the joy and satisfaction of achieving something of eternal value.

Dedicate yourself to serving the Lord and your partner for life. Then you can experience marriage in its fullest sense.

Five Stressors That Threaten Marital Partnership

While it is true that sharing your dreams can forestall some of the stress involved in building a marital partnership, several other things can create conflict, especially in the area of misguided priorities.

Vonette presents briefly some of the priority stressors that threaten to pull the average home apart.

Vonette

First, *overwork*. Bill and I have seen many couples grow apart because one partner couldn't keep his work in perspective.

If your career or ministry is causing you problems because of overwork, set stringent limits on yourself. If it is breaking up your relationship, give it up.

Your partner is the most important person in your life. When you put your career before your spouse, you may make bushels of money but you will almost certainly be miserable in the process. Ultimately, the only things that really matter in life are your relationships with the Lord, your life partner, and your family.

Busyness—a lifestyle of running from place to place, hurrying to the next project, glancing at a wristwatch every few minutes—can devastate a marriage. Your intimacy needs unhurried growth. In developing your schedule, you will be wise to place top priority on your relationship. Manage your time to give your marriage adequate attention. God doesn't want your life so packed with activity that you lack sufficient togetherness with the one you love.

Second, *family activities out of balance.* In this ministry we always place a strong emphasis on the importance of the family. We encourage fathers and mothers to be lovingly involved in the various activities of their children. At the same time we recognize that some parents in today's society are so concerned about their children that they don't give proper attention to their profession. While spending time with your family is important, sometimes family concerns can consume too much of our time and energy. To establish a proper balance, husband and wife need to constantly reevaluate and reaffirm their priorities to the Lord and to each other and the family.

We'll take a good look at God-centered priorities in the next chapter.

Third, *independent spirit.* When both husband and wife have responsible career positions, they frequently develop independent lifestyles.

Because of schedule conflicts, they attend social functions separately, have less opportunity to support each other and share less physical and emotional contact. She joins a spa; he takes up tennis. She spends her Saturday working for a charity; he goes on a fishing trip. In the meantime, they rarely pay attention to each other, and they soon slip into patterns of independent living.

Is your marriage suffering from the stress of too much self-reliance? It takes planning and commitment to overcome the handicaps of living separate lives. Schedule time together; don't expect it to "just happen." Use the telephone to keep in contact. Make it a point to include each other in decision-making. Remember, your flourishing partnership is vital to keeping your home together in a pull-apart world.

Fourth, *women as professionals.* Many women involved in high-level careers find new strains in their marital relationships. Bill and I have observed couples who have separated because their working roles destroyed their partnership.

I would encourage a professional wife to stay alert to her husband's response to her career. If their working roles contribute to an improper relationship at home, they should set definite guidelines for their partnership, and they need to continuously evaluate their responses and needs. If they find their togetherness eroding, they should immediately remedy the problem—by changing careers if necessary.

I believe it is unlikely that a couple can achieve the same level in their professions at the same time, particularly if children are involved. Generally, one partner in a supportive role is necessary and can be vital to the other.

This may be the reason that the traditional family has developed as it has—with the woman a helpmate to her husband, caring for the home, being a stay-at-home mom, nurturing the children, building relationships, and looking after the necessary details of life to free her husband to accomplish his ultimate potential. As he reaches his potential and the children mature, he gives attention to her personal achievements in addition to her accomplishments in the home. This appears, and to me has been, the most satisfying arrangement for a couple where both are high achievers and desire dual professions.

Fifth, *divided loyalties*. Perhaps you have discovered as Bill and I have that the demands of ministry, career, family, neighbors, and friends can sometimes be overwhelming. The obligations seem to stack like gridlock on a Los Angeles freeway. Schedules fall into disarray, causing conflicts, stress, and guilt. At such times it is easy to feel pulled apart by conflicting loyalties.

How do you handle your divided loyalties? Most couples manage theirs haphazardly. They respond to the "tyranny of the urgent" and ignore more important priorities. As a result, their lives become unbalanced. They feel guilty, and this provokes more conflict and uneasiness. Frustration builds and tempers flare.

Because this can develop into such a major problem, Bill shares here three suggestions that have helped us greatly in dealing with our own divided loyalties.

Bill

1. Maintain a clear perspective. If we are struggling under a cloud of condemnation, we cannot have a clear perspective of the demands on our life. It would be easy for me to feel guilty about not being able to meet all the expectations and demands of our ministry. What looms over me are my stacks of correspondence and neglected reading, and my constant deadlines on books, articles, and sermons. But I try to keep things in perspective by reminding myself that there is only so much I can do. So I do what I can, then relax. Although my days are long and meetings and conferences numerous, I have learned to cast my cares on the Lord as we have been commanded to do (1 Peter 5:7).

2. Build bridges through partnership. Spouses can reach out to each other in commitment and blend the joys and stresses of busy lifestyles to create a symphony of growth and pleasure. Even the sad, dark times will add significance to the marriage when they are experienced together by partners strongly committed to each other.

The first task in this bridge-building process is to define your loyalties and determine the priorities in your relationship. Understanding what is important to each person and what has priority will give direction and consistency to your relationship and provide a strong foundation for whatever you do. From this platform you can evaluate the demands on you and formulate a plan to deal effectively with them.

Even with a strong foundation, though, flexibility is also essential to a bridge. A few years ago, an earthquake measuring 7.1 on the Richter scale struck San Francisco. The fifteen-second temblor killed sixty-seven people and left thousands injured and homeless. Buildings, streets, and bridges suffered more than seven billion dollars in damage, making it one of the costliest natural disasters in U.S. history.

Many commuters lost their lives when the top levels of the Oakland Bay Bridge and Nimitz Freeway collapsed onto the bottom lanes. But despite the structural failure of these and other bridges in the disaster area, the famous Golden Gate Bridge survived. Why?

In this incident, the incredible ability of the bridge to flex with the tremor saved the Golden Gate. Because its roadbed rests in a massive sling of cables and spans that sway when rocked by a quake, the bridge weathered the catastrophe with little more than a superficial crack or two.

Flexing with the tremors of life will help your marriage partnership remain undamaged when divided loyalties threaten disaster. Many good resources are available to help you in this process. You could attend one of the many fine marriage seminars sponsored by Campus Crusade's FamilyLife ministry, for example. Your pastor or a professional Christian counselor can also help.

3. Cultivate a thankful attitude. This has saved the day more times than I can remember. An attitude of thankfulness has helped us tremendously in managing the stresses that threaten our partnership.

Vonette

One morning years ago I sat next to Bill, seething as he backed the car out of the driveway. How perfect we looked! The backdrop of our home was stately. As a family we were going to church. Zac and baby Brad were in sailor suits with knee socks. But I felt like a hypocrite. Outwardly the canvas was perfectly colored with correct forms, but on the back side were dark blotches of anger.

At breakfast I had tried to communicate to Bill my growing frustration over having to perform repetitive tasks. His response seemed so shallow. He called it "Spiritual Breathing," outlining how I should "exhale" a confession of my sin and "inhale" the power of the Holy Spirit by claiming God's promises by faith. I felt too out of control for such simplicity.

At church that morning I noted in the bulletin that the guest speaker's address was entitled "Looking Up." I sighed. *More weary platitudes that float above our heads.* I yearned for more substance than the allotted thirty minutes of lofty language. The speaker's opening remarks, however, felt like a prophetic word:

Dissatisfaction and frustration are not of God. If we are dissatisfied about something, we should ask God what is causing us to be that way and then ask Him to remove it. If He doesn't remove it, we are to ask what He wants us to learn from that situation.

I was deaf to any more of the speaker's words. I had been praying to be out of the Moorish castle in which we lived, or for the aid of an efficient housekeeper. I clearly knew that the Lord had not allowed either. What was He trying to teach me? Deep inside, I didn't even know if I wanted to learn, whatever it was.

The Tuesday night College Life meetings in our home were drawing enormous crowds of up to three hundred. So Bill and the staff had to push the living room and dining room furniture into auxiliary halls.

The terrible part was that I wanted to be out with the students, but I ended up spending most of the time in the kitchen preparing refreshments. It had always seemed like a mismanagement of talent; I could explain the steps to salvation with brevity and clarity, and I wanted to introduce these students to Christ. Yet, I mixed punch while younger staff members sometimes tripped in their presentation.

This particular morning, as I tried to listen to the speaker, I held my observation up to God, and He provided me with clear insight. The young staff needed the experience for training. It was as if one sliver of discontent had been extricated, and the whole wound filled with balm.

I put my arm through Bill's. It was so clearly a battle of attitude and not circumstance. I made a decision that morning to give thanks in my situation and work on performing every task as unto the Lord.

I learned the practical application of 1 Thessalonians 5:18: "No matter what happens, always be thankful, for this is God's will for you who belong to Christ Jesus" (TLB). I began to thank God for the dishes, the diapers, the dust, and the drudgery. The result was amazing. I began to find joy in the tasks that I had formerly resented. I experienced a new sense of victory and excitement in living for and serving Christ. And that threat to our partnership was totally disarmed.

Perhaps you can think of a time in your life when giving thanks has quieted the storm of conflicting demands upon you. I have learned that, whenever I respond to conflict with a thankful attitude, the demands roaring at me are muzzled. Their voices diminish until I can sort them out and deal with them one by one.

Bill

Both Vonette and I encourage you to maintain a clear perspective on the daily pressures that threaten your partnership. The key is to see yourself and your spouse as partners in life, then construct flexible bridges across the chasms of your differences. Ask the Holy Spirit to help you develop the habit of a thankful attitude. These three suggestions will combine to help bring you to a partnership in which you can trust, and they will lead you to a more intimate, joyful, Spirit-filled marriage.

By following these principles and taking the next step in building a godly home, you will learn how to prevent or reduce many of the stresses in your relationship.

ટ**

For Reflection, Discussion, and Action

1. Amos 3:3 asks, "Can two walk together, unless they are agreed?" (NKJ). How can you and your spouse improve your walk together? Discuss with your partner.

2. What dream do you and your spouse share? How have you verbally expressed that dream to your mate?

3. This week, at the end of each day, jot down in a notebook the number of hours that you spent: (a) doing work-related tasks; (b) being with your children; (c) being exclusively with your spouse; and (d) praying and meditating on God's Word. Will you adjust your schedule for next week? How?

4. A dual career produces divided loyalties. Describe the divided loyalties that you have experienced. How has this affected your marriage partnership?

5. Flexibility and compromise are effective tools for handling divided loyalties. Describe how you plan to use these tools to manage your marriage partnership.

Step 2

Establish God-Centered Priorities

ॐ

Priorities are like roads on a well-marked map. The main priority thoroughfare is a vital spiritual life. The second major route is godly stewardship of our time, talents, and treasure.

Chapter 3

Step 2: Establish God-Centered Priorities

❧

WHEN THE Crystal Palace Exhibition opened in 1851, people flocked to London's Hyde Park to view the marvels. Steam power had captured the imagination of inventors. Lines of people gaped at the steam plows, steam locomotives, steam looms, steam organs, and even a steam cannon.

But first prize went to an exhibit that defied description. It boasted 7,000 moving parts. Its pulleys clanked, whistles shrieked, bells clanged, and gears ground, all making an incredible noise. But the contraption didn't do a thing. In spite of the motion and commotion, the machine had no practical use.

Have you ever felt like that machine? Spinning countless plans and whirling through innumerable projects, but accomplishing little? Sometimes it is easy to fool ourselves by mistaking activity for achievement.

Perhaps you have experienced this in your marriage. Your relationship wins a blue ribbon in the eyes of others, but you realize that your goals and dreams are being shattered by frenzied activity. You frequently become side-tracked from doing what you and your spouse agree is best for your unity.

Setting Priorities

Vonette and I want to share some practical principles that we are convinced will bring purpose and great rewards to your marriage as they have ours: how you can build godly attitudes and establish God-centered priorities that will help you build your home more effectively.

Priorities are like roads on a well-marked map pointing the way to our destination. Let us look at the Christian couple's roadmap for a moment.

The main priority thoroughfare is *a vital spiritual life*. This includes a dynamic, personal walk with our Savior and Lord, Jesus Christ. It also includes a godly communion with your spouse. Surrendering to the Lordship of Christ and living through the power of the Holy Spirit enables you to set and enjoy God-centered priorities.

The second major route on the map of priorities is *godly stewardship*. God has entrusted you with the resources you need for a successful marriage. By following biblical prin-ciples for stewardship, you will experience less friction in your relationship.

Let us consider these in more depth.

A Vital Spiritual Life

Vonette and I have found that to enjoy a strong and inti-mate partnership, we must put God first in our marriage. We must surrender absolutely to the Lordship of Christ. We must yield totally to the control of the Holy Spirit.

Let me illustrate. One evening I spoke to several hundred couples. As I stood behind the lectern, I noticed one particularly attractive couple sitting close to the front on my left. The woman held her head confidently, and had fine, classical features. The man's rough-hewn looks complemented hers.

After I finished my talk, this couple rushed up to me. When the crowd thinned, we sat together in a corner of the room.

"We're planning to get a divorce," the young man explained immediately.

His remark caught me by surprise. "Tell me a little about yourselves."

"We've been married two years and have worked in Christian ministry the entire time," the young woman began with a note of sadness in her voice.

I looked at her. "That sounds like an exciting life. What's the problem?"

"I don't like my wife's looks," the man blurted impatiently.

Surprised, I laughed. It was one of the most ridiculous statements he could have made.

"What are you laughing about?" he muttered, offended.

"Your wife is a beautiful woman. I can't imagine why you would say you don't like her appearance."

Apparently, that young husband was letting sinful thoughts ruin his love for his wife. Even though he wanted his marriage to succeed, his mindset was distorting their relationship.

I explained that every Christian has two natures: The Bible describes one as the "old man" or "the flesh." The other is called the "new man," representing the person who walks in the power of the Holy Spirit.

I took a sheet of paper and began drawing the following diagram:

Our Control Center

God

Satan

"This circle," I explained, "represents what I call the throne room in your life. The chair symbolizes a throne— the control center. There are two spiritual kingdoms seeking to influence us. One is God's kingdom and the other is Satan's. Before we became Christians, as members of Satan's kingdom, we had no choice but to yield to his influence. But when we received Christ, we surrendered our 'control center' to Him."

Then I added to the diagram:

Freedom of Choice

God

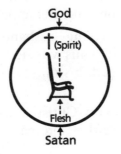

Satan

To explain the additions, I asked both of them to turn in their Bibles to Galatians 5:16,17. "Here," I pointed out, "the apostle Paul describes the ongoing conflict that takes place between the kingdom of God and the kingdom of Satan."

I advise you to obey only the Holy Spirit's instructions. He will tell you where to go and what to do, and then you won't always be doing the wrong things your evil nature wants you to.

For we naturally love to do evil things that are just the opposite from the things that the Holy Spirit tells us to do; and the good things we want to do when the spirit has his way with us are just the opposite of our natural desires. These two forces within us are constantly fighting each other to win control over us, and our wishes are never free from their pressures (TLB).

"Our two natures, the spirit and the flesh," I continued, "battle one another for our attention. God gives us freedom of choice, and we often allow the flesh to retake the throne."

I turned to the young man. "Which nature do you suppose is responsible for your critical attitude concerning your wife?"

"The flesh," he sighed.

"Who is the source of the ways of the flesh?"

He studied the diagram. "Satan."

"So when you agree with those negative thoughts about your wife, whom are you allowing to control you?"

His face turned white. "Satan."

I continued. "Satan has no power to break up marriages. He does, however, have the ability to tempt and entice us with every kind of evil. We have the choice to say yes or no to his clever, subtle, and devious temptations.

"When we as Christians live in sin, we are still in God's possession but we have yielded to the influence of Satan and given control of the throne to the flesh," I explained. "Christ is no longer on the throne, but He continually seeks to influence us and bring us back to God's ways. As long as we allow our self-centered, fleshly nature to remain on the throne, our attitudes and actions will be selfish and sinful."

I added a radio dial to the diagram:

Making the Right Choice

"We have the choice of whether to listen to Satan's lies or to God," I explained. "We can consciously decide to 'turn the dial,' as on a radio, and listen to a better program—God's program! And God's program is to help you love your wife with your whole heart. What would you like to do?"

"Turn the dial." His face broke into a Cheshire grin.

So we bowed in prayer and committed his new attitude to the Lord.

When I happened to see the couple an hour later, he said, "She looks better to me already." He grinned and hugged her.

She smiled with pleasure.

Six months later, I was walking across the campus when I observed a couple swinging hands and looking at each other with adoring glances. Suddenly, we recognized each other. It was this same couple. They exclaimed over and over how much they appreciated my counsel at our previous meeting.

"We have been using the diagram that you shared with us to help other people with marital problems," he enthused.

"It can also help people with just about any problem," she chimed in.

Through the years, I have explained this diagram of the throne to millions of people. I know of no better way to deal with temptation and conflict. And I have applied its life-changing truth to my own life. A daily "Throne Check," as I call it, is crucial to maintaining God-centered priorities and a vital spiritual life. It's what keeps Vonette and me on the road to marital harmony.

Godly Stewardship

Now we are ready to look at that map again, this time at the second road leading to a godly home. If our goal is to prevent unnecessary conflict or reduce the potential for friction in our relationship, we must agree on basic principles of *godly stewardship* of time, talent, and treasure (finances).[1]

---

[1] For more information on these principles, I encourage you to read my Transferable Concept, *How You Can Experience the Adventure of Giving* (NewLife Publications).

A steward is someone who oversees the affairs of a household or estate, or manages the accounts and property of another person.

A *faithful* steward manages his own time, talent, and treasure for maximum effectiveness in doing God's will.

Vonette and I have discovered that good stewardship of our time, talent, and treasure is foundational for handling the stressors that pull a home apart. The whole of life—our personality, influence, material substance, and especially our family—is His, and He holds us accountable for what He has given us (Matthew 25:14–20; Romans 14:12). We will discuss stewardship more fully in the next chapter.

We encourage you to dedicate all of your resources—your time and talents as well as your finances—to the Lordship of Jesus Christ. Commit yourselves together to prayer and God's Word. Make fellowship with the Lord the center of your day. Walk with Him and talk with Him continuously. Your trust in God will help you keep in perspective the demands and strains you face, and it will enable you to build a lasting partnership more easily.

Build on your partnership and watch how your oneness adds to your abilities. Find the security and comfort of having that one special person who will help you develop your talents and share your successes for a lifetime.

The principle of godly stewardship is founded on the premise that God is the source and owner of all we possess. All that we have, we own under God. He has put into our hands the administration of all that He owns. Over the years, we have learned that putting God first in our time, talents, and treasure must be the goal of our stewardship. Once this is accomplished, all else falls into place.

The first step in godly stewardship is to accept God's ownership over your life and all that you possess. Dedicate your time, talents, and treasure, to Him without reservation. Let's take a closer look at each of these.

First, *manage your time.* How many times have you heard this philosophy: "Time is money"? Christians have sayings, too—one is: "Every minute must count for the Lord."

While we need not be working every minute, we do need to realize that our time is different from that of non-Christians. It all belongs to our Lord. None of it is free time. When He redeemed us, He bought it all.

And He expects us to be good stewards of it. God knows just how much time we have, and there is always enough to do all that He wants us to do.

> *The principle of godly stewardship is founded on the premise that God is the source and owner of all we possess.*
>
> 🕊

We find, though, that there is never enough time to do what God wants, *plus* what we want if what we want conflicts with His desires. This represents a plurality of priorities, and these steal your time and add to the stresses in your life. When you determine your priorities according to what the Lord wants you to do, you demonstrate good stewardship of your time and relieve some of your stress.

Early in my Christian experience, I learned that one secret to preventing stress in the use of time is, again, to cast all our cares on the Lord, as He leads us to do in 1 Peter 5:7.

In managing our time effectively, we can depend on the wisdom of the Holy Spirit to guide us as we pray the words of Psalm 90:12: "So teach us to number our days, that we may present to Thee a heart of wisdom."

Second, *manage your talents.* God has given each of us at least one special ability. We would be poor stewards if we ignored that talent. God expects us to develop our gift to its fullest potential through the control and empowering of the Holy Spirit. Failing to do so leaves us feeling frustrated and unfulfilled.

Sometimes, however, we can over-commit ourselves in using our talents. A husband's expertise, for example, may lie in financial management—but he spends too many hours helping the church with its annual budget. A wife's gift in music may take her away from her family too many weekends as she performs in concerts.

A faithful steward maximizes his abilities for God's glory. God is pleased when we encourage each other to use our talents. But He doesn't expect us to neglect our greatest gift—each other—in the process.

Third, *manage your treasure.* Much sorrow in marriage stems from a lack of understanding and a failure to apply the principles of financial stewardship.

Vonette and I discovered early in our marriage that resolving financial differences begins with spiritual commitment. On a Sunday afternoon in the spring of 1951, we decided to seal our commitment in a contract with the Lord.

As a businessman, I had signed hundreds of contracts. From my perspective, it seemed reasonable to make an agreement between us and the Lord, too. Vonette seemed to catch my fervor. "You mean, sign it and everything?"

I started to clear the kitchen table where we had just finished lunch. "Yes, let's do it this afternoon. Let's write down exactly what we want out of life. Our lifetime goals. And put the contract where we both can see it."

"Yes, let's do it," Vonette enthused.

We went into separate rooms in our home in the Hollywood hills and got down on our knees to spend time alone with our Lord in prayer. We each determined to follow the example of Jesus who said that He always did what pleased the Father, and the example of the apostle Paul who referred to himself as a "slave" of Jesus Christ (Romans 1:1, TLB).

We realized that this was to be the most important agreement of our lives. Individually and as a couple we were surrendering ourselves totally to the Lord Jesus Christ to become His "slaves" forever.

In the contract, we vowed not to seek personal wealth, success, praise, honor, or power for ourselves. Our document, which each of us signed, went something like this:

From this day, Lord, we surrender and relinquish all of our past, present, and future rights and material possessions to you. As an act of the will, by faith, we choose to become Your bondslaves and do whatever You want us to do, go wherever You want us to go, say whatever You want us to say, no matter what it costs, for the rest of our lives. With Your help, we will never again seek the praise or applause of men or the material wealth of the world.

That agreement has been the foundation for our lives and ministry ever since. We have never regretted surrendering our lives and possessions completely and irrevocably to our Lord. As a result, Vonette and I personally own little of this world's goods. Yet we have always abundantly enjoyed the blessings of God that he promised to all who trust and obey Him. On thousands of occasions we have experienced the faithfulness of God to meet our every need above and beyond our fondest hopes and desires.

Just because we have made these choices in regard to material possessions does not mean that we suggest you do the same. But we encourage you to seek God and do as He directs you.

We would like to share several guidelines that will help you be a good steward of your own resources.

First, *accept God's ownership.* The first step in godly stewardship is to accept God's ownership over your lives and all that you possess. Surrender your time and talents, as well as your treasures, to Him without reservation.

List your financial priorities according to biblical principles. Make the items clear and specific so you can easily follow them in your daily living. Discuss the major areas in which you disagree and ask the Holy Spirit to show you how to resolve them.

Second, *see your spouse as a partner.* Partnership in stewardship is essential to marital harmony. Vonette and I believe, for example, that the most capable spouse should handle the money. Once you have set priorities and decided how to handle your finances, delegate the responsibility to the partner who has the best aptitude or the most time available for bookkeeping.

Praying together and following the leadership of the Holy Spirit, we have learned, is essential for financial agreement. We recommend that when disagreements come, you get down on your knees and pray together. Ask God to give you His wisdom and direction. If you still can't come together on the issue, declare a moratorium for twenty-four hours. Don't discuss the situation with each other. Talk to the Lord; ask Him to give you further insight.

If you still can't resolve the problem, try the moratorium for another twenty-four hours. For a crucial issue, we suggest that you pray *and* fast. Do a Throne Check and allow God to speak to you. Examine your motives. If done with honesty, this will help you identify problems and find creative solutions.

Third, *follow biblical guidelines for giving*. God's provision is based on the law of the harvest: "A man reaps what he sows" (Galatians 6:7, NIV). From the seed of your giving, God will enable you to harvest bountiful fruit.

Tithing—giving at least a tenth of our income or resources to God—serves as a practical guideline for giving and ensures consistent stewardship. Without a functional plan for giving, it is easy to fall prey to the emotions and circumstances that hinder you from being faithful stewards.

Since everything still belongs to God, tithing teaches us to put Him first. God does not honor a gift that comes from leftovers. He requires the first and the best of our increase (Exodus 22:29,30). Putting God first releases us from the tyranny of materialism and clears the channel for God's continued abundant blessings (2 Timothy 2:4).

Fourth, *live in financial freedom.* So many couples succumb to the lure of materialism. But our Lord commands us to be free from financial bondage. We need to adopt a reasonably simple lifestyle and focus our finances on our needs, not our greeds. We are to wear the cloak of materialism loosely.

I recognize that we do not all share the same view of a "simple lifestyle." Ask the Lord how He wants you to define it. Jesus promised a full and abundant life to all who trust and obey Him. God wants us to enjoy pleasure and convenience. It is how we use and share our possessions that counts. Use everything to God's honor and glory and you will thwart the temptation to buy unnecessary items.

Let me suggest a simple formula that can help you live in financial freedom: Give at least the first 10 percent of your income to God and invest a second 10 percent for emergencies and retirement. Then live on the remaining 80 percent. If this is not possible for you, decide on a percentage for your "savings" that fits your budget.

When Christ is on the throne of our lives, we have no difficulty accepting our God-given stewardship over all of life. We see our possessions as God's gift to make us successful in ministry. By following the biblical pattern of giving, we will significantly reduce the daily stress caused by last-minute, crisis-initiated decision-making.

૨૦

For Reflection, Discussion, and Action

1. Have you used the Throne Check to prevent potential problems in your marriage? If this concept is new to you, how will you utilize it? (Identify a specific problem area in your marriage as an example.)

2. If you and your spouse have not done so, surrender your time, talents, and financial resources to the Lord. You may want to make a written contract.

3. To whom have you delegated the bookkeeping responsibilities in your marriage? Why?

4. Sit down together and look over your checkbook. Are you, as a couple, following biblical guidelines for giving? If not, how will you make adjustments to correct this situation?

Step 3

Develop
"Other-Centeredness"

❧

*Through praise, communication, and
a healthy sex life, couples develop a
sense of "other-centeredness" that enables
them to achieve greater wholeness and
intimacy in their relationship.*

Chapter 4

Step 3: Develop "Other-Centeredness"

 география

THROUGH PRAISE, communication, and a healthy sex life, couples develop a sense of "other-centeredness" that enables them to achieve greater wholeness and intimacy in their relationship.

During Explo '85, I was in West Berlin on our thirty-seventh wedding anniversary. Vonette was in London in the video control studio that coordinated the transmission of our television broadcasts around the world via eighteen satellites.

As I stood before the packed house in the Internationalen Kongresszentrum, I remembered that this was our anniversary. On impulse, I decided to give a special anniversary greeting to Vonette. My words were carried live over our worldwide television network to more than 250,000 people in 98 auditoriums with millions more listening in by television.

"Before I bring my message today, I want to take a moment to wish my beautiful, adorable wife of thirty-seven years a happy anniversary." The crowd went wild as

I told her how much I loved and appreciated her. Cameras in the control studio in London caught her surprised reaction and broadcast it. What a spectacular joy that was for me and the entire worldwide audience to witness her surprise and amazement.

Vonette

I was thrilled to hear Bill's declaration of love on worldwide television. That was quite a public demonstration of his affection for me.

Later, when he spoke in Mexico City for the final event of the tour, he learned that many people had wept when they viewed the earlier broadcast. What touched them most was when they saw Bill's love for me after all these years. Someone mentioned later that, as a result of seeing the broadcast, he had praised his wife and lifted the world.

Praise is an expression of our devotion to our mate. It is the channel through which we communicate our appreciation and gratitude for each other. It is the means by which we exchange honor and respect. It is one way we share our other-centeredness.

No marriage can succeed if either spouse insists on taking center stage. Consciously looking first to the welfare of our partner enables us to open ourselves to each other. We call this focus having a sense of other-centeredness.

Other-centeredness is a basic scriptural principle. The apostle Paul urges all Christians, "Love each other with brotherly affection and take delight in honoring each other" (Romans 12:10, TLB). In Ephesians, he describes how this precept applies to marital love: "Husbands should love their wives as their own bodies...For no man ever hates his own flesh, but nourishes and cherishes it, as Christ does the church" (Ephesians 5:28,29, RSV).

That's quite a comparison! We go to great lengths to care for ourselves. Store shelves are filled with items to make us look younger and feel better. The food we eat, the clothes we buy, the way we spend our time, all focus on satisfying our own needs and desires. If we were to give as much attention to our mate as we do to the care of our own bodies, our marriage would dramatically blossom with blessings.

Bill

A sense of other-centeredness is absolutely necessary for a healthy marital relationship. In this chapter, Vonette and I want to share three ways you can establish and strengthen your sense of other-centeredness and achieve greater intimacy in your relationship.

The Selfless Qualities of Praise

Praise as a lifestyle, first to God and then to our mate, cleanses us from self-centeredness. It opens channels of communication, builds unity and harmony, enhances our mate's self-esteem, and gives energy to our partnership.

Vonette and I keep our channel of communication open in many ways, but let me give you one example. Sometimes she expresses her displeasure over something I shouldn't have done. Instead of being confrontational, I have learned to respond with a compliment. "I'm the most fortunate man in the world to have such a wonderful wife," I smile. And I tell her how much I appreciate her for putting up with me and whatever it is I may be doing to irritate her. This kind of response, we have found, disarms a potentially tense situation and keeps our communication open.

By practicing lifestyle praise to God and to each other, we have discovered that divisions between us vanish and peace is restored.

The reason is simple.

Giving thanks transforms our negative dispositions into positive attitudes. I truly believe that praise encourages us to cherish each other, to focus on the positives in our relationship, thus building harmony and strengthening our marital bonds.

This helps build self-esteem.

Vonette

Genuine praise always lifts those around us. When Bill expresses his appreciation for me, I feel good about myself. I have more confidence and self-respect. When I praise Bill in public, I draw attention to his strengths and abilities. Others form favorable opinions about him. This too helps build his self-esteem.

> *Just as praise energizes our relationship with our heavenly Father, so praise of our spouse gives energy to our partnership.*
>
> ❧

Just as praise energizes our relationship with our heavenly Father, so praise of our spouse gives energy to our partnership.

During Explo '85, Bill traveled more than 40,000 miles in four-and-a-half days and spoke twenty times. I stayed in London to help coordinate the leadership strategy.

Shortly after each daily broadcast, Bill would call. Each

time I would encourage him, "You're doing a great job." Then he would fly to the next engagement on another continent.

I came home after the event expecting to find Bill exhausted. I was surprised to find him cheerful and invigorated.

"I'm so thrilled over everything that has happened," he enthused. "My last message was my best. I seemed to gather strength and energy as I traveled. You don't know how much I appreciate the encouragement you gave me all along the way."

Bill

Praise is contagious. Whenever I affirm Vonette, not only do I brighten her life, but mine as well. The dynamic energy we create keeps our relationship intimate and vital.

Here are three practical steps you can take to make praise a way of life and reduce the stress in your marriage:

First, *find qualities worthy of praise.* I encourage you to search out qualities in your mate that are worthy of praise. Think about it. Is your husband dedicated to his job? Does he help around the house without being asked? Does your wife fix your favorite meal? Has she accomplished a significant task on her job? Does she look particularly attractive today? Keep these characteristics fresh in your mind. Let them supplant any temptation to criticize or tear down.

Second, *show gratitude regularly.* How long does your partner wait between compliments? How many times have you neglected showing appreciation for a kindness he has shown to you?

I encourage you to show gratitude to your partner regularly. Be creative. Look for the ways he serves you and express your thanks.

Third, *offer a sacrifice of praise*. Sometimes praise calls for sacrifice. The apostle Paul admonishes: "By Him [Jesus Christ] let us continually offer the sacrifice of praise to God, that is, the fruit of our lips, giving thanks to His name" (Hebrews 13:15, NKJ). This applies to our marriage relationship as well.

Many spouses affirm each other only when it's convenient or when things are going well. But praise means so much more when it is offered during difficult times—when we are in sorrow, suffering pain, experiencing loneliness, or in the midst of stressful and harried circumstances. Praise that springs sacrificially from our innermost being pleases God and enriches our marriage.

Intimacy Through Communication

Praise is but the first step in establishing and maintaining your intimacy. Vonette and I have discovered another valuable secret.

Think back to the early days of your courtship for a moment. Remember how you would sit across from each other in a restaurant, gaze into each other's eyes, and talk for hours about your hopes and dreams?

I remember how reluctant Vonette and I were to say goodnight after a date. We had so much more to talk about.

All too often, after the initial excitement of marriage wears off, husbands and wives let their intimacy decline into dull routine. As a couple who has been happily married since 1948, we know you can restore that lost sparkle of intimacy and enrich your sense of other-centeredness if you really want to.

We want to share with you the principles that have helped us build intimacy through communication.

Many couples equate intimacy with romance and sex. But intimacy is more than this. It is a process of sharing our total selves with our partner. It includes seeking to understand the inner and outer nature of our spouse. It means revealing our most private self and giving freely of our body, mind, and spirit. Intimacy comes when we know our mate thoroughly, yet love him or her faithfully.

Shared values and experiences, vulnerability, a sense of safety, sensitivity, loyalty, communication, forgiveness, and prayer form the building blocks of closeness. The foundation upon which these qualities rest, however, is our common faith in God that allows us to risk trusting each other.

Building intimacy is a lifetime commitment that requires openness and work. But the adventure is worth every moment because intimacy creates a joyful oneness of heart and mind.

The cornerstone of marital intimacy is open and loving communication. Does your relationship provide a safe haven for communication on the deepest spiritual and emotional level? Do you and your spouse freely share your dreams? Your fears? Your failures? Your successes? Can you weep together as well as laugh together? Do you support each other in crisis or pain?

For you "macho" men who would rather spend hours watching football or going hunting for days with your buddies, this may seem a difficult challenge. Yet we cannot build intimacy without such communication.

Let me briefly share with you six principles that will help you build intimacy through communication.

First, *listen*. Each of us has a deep need to be heard and understood. We want to share our thoughts, feelings, and ideas. But communication is first listening.

When we truly listen to our partner, we give of ourselves and focus on our mate. As you and your partner talk together, give your undivided attention and don't interrupt unless necessary.

In the past I would read a newspaper while Vonette talked. When she got upset, I would tease her. "I have two eyes and two ears. I can do several things at once. I am listening."

But one day she turned the tables on me. And when I couldn't get her attention, I didn't appreciate it one bit. Now I understand how much she needs my total attention when she has something to say to me. Ever since, we have made a joke about getting one another's undivided attention.

Men, provide your wife with a safe harbor for sharing her concerns. Resist the temptation to use this respite for romance or sex. Simply commit yourself to listening. You may find that this means going to a neutral place like a restaurant so your wife is free from normal distractions.

Second, *speak gently*. I hate to throw anything away, even socks—especially if they are my favorite. One morning I slipped on a pair that had a weak elastic top. So I used a safety pin to hold one up.

Vonette's sharp eye noticed it. "Why are you wearing a safety pin in your sock?"

"The elastic's loose."

"Why don't you throw them away?"

"But I've worn them for fifteen years. They've become my friends."

She laughed. "Well, Bill Bright, after fifteen years they deserve to be retired! It wouldn't be worth my time to fix them. If I sewed elastic inside the sock, you wouldn't wear it."

"But they're still good socks!" I insisted. "They don't have any holes. The only problem is, they droop."

To me, pinning up a prize sock was no big deal. But to Vonette, her value as a wife was at stake. She looked at my sock and thought, *Oh, man, that makes me feel guilty.* To have a pin in my sock signaled to her that Bill Bright needed attention.

For many couples, such differences in values could turn conversations into angry confrontations. Words can inflict pain, unless we speak them gently—and sometimes with humor. Vonette and I have smoothed many potential conflicts in our relationship with humor and by being gentle in our responses.

Third, *communicate through touch.* Touching says what words cannot.

When Vonette rubs my back, I feel special and respond like a cat having his fur stroked. If we sit near each other, we move closer to share our oneness.

Each morning and evening when we are together, we humble ourselves before God on our knees. We often hold hands when we pray to signify our unity. Vonette's warm embrace during sad experiences brings more comfort than a thousand words.

The necessity of nonsexual touching continues throughout marriage. We encourage you to find unique ways of communicating with your spouse through touch. Ask your partner for positive physical contact when you need it.

Fourth, *be vulnerable.* To be vulnerable we must risk revealing who we are. This isn't easy.

Keep yourself open to your partner. Accept the pain and inconvenience you may feel from your vulnerability as part of the process of building your relationship.

Fifth, *forgive freely*. Genuine forgiveness is more than pretending an offense didn't happen. It is an act of the will, in the power of the Holy Spirit, by which we release another from owing us anything because of his offense and we surrender the hurt to God.

Forgiveness resolves the conflicts in our relationship. It helps us respond lovingly to criticism and listen to our spouse's negative remarks and learn from them. As a result, we answer calmly and quietly, rather than fueling the flame of ill feelings.

Sixth, *pray together*. For many years Vonette and I have slept in two double beds brought together by a single headboard made by my brother. I sleep in one bed, she in the other. But every night before we go to sleep, we kneel to pray together. Once in bed, I usually stay beside her until she falls asleep. Then I move easily back to my bed. When we awake each morning, we kneel to pray as we ask our risen Lord to continue living His resurrection life in and through us.

Our prayer life has increased intimacy in our communication. Our relationship helps us to pray more intelligently for each other's walk with the heavenly Father. We could not imagine intimacy without the cleansing power of talking to our Lord together.

We encourage you to develop the practice of praying together. If in the course of the day you become impatient with each other, ask your spouse for forgiveness before you pray together at night. Invite the Holy Spirit to help you communicate clearly and lovingly. Discover the innermost secrets of your hearts together through communion with the heavenly Father.

We work at communicating wherever we are. And one of the most exciting avenues of intimate communication is through our sexual relationship. The communication we have developed through the years helps us to enjoy that area of our lives even more today than when we first married.

Sex: God's Gift for Other-Centeredness

Vonette and I now are at the stage of life we used to think was too old for people to have ideas about sex. Not only do we still have ideas, we celebrate our sexuality regularly.

In fact, we are experiencing a richer, fuller sex life now than at any time in our forty-plus years together. The ways we have grown together have helped to make our physical relationship what it is today.

Sex should be the most intimate experience in the marriage relationship. All the other qualities of a successful marriage—emotional intimacy, partnership, and communication—contribute to a healthy sex life, making it the ultimate celebration, the icing on the cake.

Sex was God's idea from the beginning. He created the human body with its desires and called it good. He did not make certain parts of our nature honorable and others evil.

God's Word talks about sexual intercourse simply as that Adam "knew" Eve (Genesis 4:1, NKJ). This implies the most intimate knowledge of a partner possible. God understood the beauty of getting to know one person in a deeply intimate way and formed us to express our romantic love physically.

But romantic love is more than physical. Our sexual and spiritual lives are linked. The marriage bond between a husband and wife symbolizes a believer's spiritual union with our Lord Jesus Christ (Ephesians 5:23,25,26,31,32).

The sexual side of marriage is the culmination of marital partnership. Nowhere else do we express our unity more fully than through this union. Both partners become givers and receivers. Their relationship attains its highest meaning and beauty when they offer their partnership to God who brought them together as one.

Because sex bonds a couple spiritually as well as physically, they share more than a moment of pleasure; they experience a wholeness in their relationship that only the Spirit of God can create. Sex outside of marriage violates the law of God, grieves the Holy Spirit, and robs the participants of this blessedness.

Have you ever thought, *Our sex life is so routine, I can predict every second of our time together?* Or, *Our sex life lost its magic years ago?*

Like anything else in marriage, physical affection takes time and thought. Vonette shares valuable insight on how you can keep the romance alive in your marriage:

Vonette

1. Make the bedroom the most beautiful room in the house. Decorate it with feminine touches and loveliness. Don't use the bedroom as a study or workroom. Instead, reserve this special place as a fun and secure haven for the two of you.

2. Wives, wear feminine nightclothes. Negligees should be among the most lovely and special pieces in your wardrobe. Save your favorite gown for romantic evenings to heighten your sense of awareness every time you put it on.

3. Take every precaution for good daily hygiene. Nothing cools a romantic feeling more than unpleasant body odors, bad breath, or uncleanliness. Use your regimen to entice your partner.

4. Create a romantic atmosphere. Bill and I have found that romantic music, flowers, soft lights, fresh linen, perfume, and other thoughtful touches in decor really do make a difference.

5. Be creative. Avoid the sameness in your lovemaking. Imagine new ways to give your partner enjoyment. Study your mate to discover the little things that turn his sexual experience into the most pleasure. Prepare ahead of time for those special touches that make him tingle and feel loved.

6. Deal with negative feelings before you enter the bedroom. Depression, anger, resentment, or selfishness will thwart your sexual intimacy. Build time into your evening to talk over your problems. Use the Throne Check. Keep channels of communication open during your time together by practicing forgiveness and by supporting and nurturing your partner.

7. Balance sexual desire with companionship. Keep in touch when you are apart. Whenever possible, call your mate at least once a day just to say, "I love you." Bill has done this for years. If for some reason he has not called me by noon, I call him. Wives, don't wait for him to take the initiative. When he travels, anticipate your reunion. Plan for his return by fixing his favorite meal or buying a small gift. Husbands, when you are away, send romantic cards and shop for special gifts that express your love but are not necessarily expensive.

8. Keep humor in your relationship. Bill has a way of disarming me with his sense of humor. One day I pointed out—maybe a little too harshly—"You spilled gravy on your tie!"

A sly look crept across his face. "I don't think a wife should be critical of her husband when he gets food on his tie," he responded. "All he has to do is put the tie in the refrigerator to keep the food from spoiling."

How could I stay irritated? I had to laugh.

9. Do special things for each other. You can do many little things for your partner. If his shirts need buttons, sew them on. Take the time to prepare a candlelight dinner. Fix breakfast and bring it to your spouse in bed. Use timely bits of praise and communication to deepen your intimacy.

Surprise does wonders to romance as well. Bring home flowers. Buy a favorite perfume or cologne. Take your spouse on a mystery date. The list of surprises is endless. Unexpected pleasures and deeds will heighten your anticipation of sex immensely.

10. Play together. A dear friend led a very disciplined life. He read his Bible daily, jogged regularly, and worked hard. But his schedule left no room for his wife's needs. Finally, his marriage virtually crumbled.

Realizing his error, he rearranged his schedule. He studied his Bible at a more convenient time. He cut down on the time he spent exercising. Although he continued to work hard, he began to spend time at home doing fun things with his wife.

Their nonsexual play soon increased their desire for each other, and their sexual life began to improve dramatically.

Bill

Companionship is expressed in showing respect for your partner. Belittling each other—in private or in public—inhibits sexual intimacy. Be sensitive to the moods and feelings of your mate. Make your partner your best friend, in the bedroom and out.

Don't violate your partner's trust. Vonette and I have a rule when we travel: Neither of us spends time alone with someone of the opposite sex. No matter where we are, we don't show undue affection for anyone else. And, if necessary, we gently rebuff any unseemly actions from others.

We have committed ourselves to remain faithful to each other until death. I tell Vonette, "I'd rather die than be unfaithful to you." And she knows I mean it. On countless occasions I have prayed, "Father, if there is a chance that I will bring dishonor to You by being unfaithful to Vonette, please take my life first." God knows I mean that prayer.

We have discovered that our sexual relationship demands our deepest commitment to each other. But the benefits we receive—a secure partnership, firmly established priorities, and a thriving intimacy—bring great satisfaction and enable us to reduce the stresses we experience.

So far we have presented three of the four steps for building a home in a pull-apart world: *Enter into a partnership; establish God-centered priorities;* and *develop other-centeredness.* In the coming pages, we will discuss another step that will help you manage the stresses of parenting: *Build a godly home for your family.* These principles will help you understand better how to hang tough in family crises.

❧

For Reflection, Discussion, and Action

1. Praise is the natural expression of love. Find five things worthy of praise in your spouse and share them.

2. Review the principles for building intimacy. What role does communication play in your relationship?

3. List several suggestions on how a spouse can become a good listener. How have you applied these in your marriage?

4. Give examples of how you are building intimacy with your spouse.

5. What creative ideas can you employ to keep the romance in your relationship despite your busy schedule?

6. Trust and intimacy are closely linked. What elements in your marriage could be preventing the growth of trust and intimacy?

Step 4

Build a Godly Home for Your Family

When couples accept their children as God's plan for their child-rearing years, they can hang tough through family crises and keep their relationship vibrant during extended periods of stress.

Chapter 5

Step 4: Build a Godly Home for Your Family

☙

JUST AS WE were ready to leave, a famous coach—who had traveled across the country to California to participate in the New Year's Day Rose Bowl game—arrived at Arrowhead Springs unannounced. He had driven all the way from Pasadena just to chat with me.

I faced a real dilemma. I wanted to visit with this great coach, whom I truly admired, but I also wanted to spend time with my sons. I had promised to take them for an afternoon of fun in the snow of the San Bernardino mountains. Should I tell him that I didn't have time and risk offending him? Or should I put the boys off until another day?

Parenting children in a busy household poses special problems. The tension between ministry or business demands and the children's need for loving attention frequently places burdens on the family. Working couples often must juggle responsibilities and decide issues not faced by traditional families. They have less time and energy to spend in rearing their children. A colicky baby, a hyperactive child, or a troublesome teenager can significantly increase the pressure on them. Soon their partnership suffers and the family feels the consequences.

Did you feel about parenting as I did before the arrival of our first child? Did you have idealistic lists of "do's and don'ts" to turn out well-adjusted, mature young adults? How terrifying it must have seemed when few of those "do's and don'ts" actually applied.

Many prospective parents fail to realize that parenting is at least a twenty-year task involving intensive work and attention. Expecting to adjust easily to the little one joining their twosome, they don't prepare adequately for extensive changes. Soon they are knee-deep in diapers, bottles, and babysitters' telephone numbers. They can't see an end in sight, and wonder how they could have stumbled into such a pressure-filled lifestyle.

Coping With the Stress of Parenting

Vonette and I have found the challenges of parenting not only surmountable but have used them to enrich our family life. She shares six practical guidelines that will help you build a godly home for your family.

Vonette

First, *realize that children are a gift of God.* In today's pull-apart world, many parents regard their children as nuisances. But God's Word says, "Children are a gift from God; they are his reward" (Psalm 127:3, TLB). Although children often cause stressful moments in our lives, seeing them as God's gifts and not nuisances to push aside gives us a godly and positive perspective on parenting.

Second, *give your partner top priority.* Nothing builds security for children more than a loving relationship between their parents. Your child's most fundamental sense of love and security will come from watching how you and your spouse relate to each other.

A nurturing marital partnership provides fertile soil for your child to grow and achieve independence. He should have no doubt that your spouse is the number one person in your life, aside from the Lord Jesus.

Third, *trust God with your children.* Entrusting God with your children will help defuse the anxiety you feel over their future and enable you to react in difficult situations with a godly perspective.

When Zac and Brad were small, Bill and I often heard stories about how children of other Christian leaders didn't follow the Lord. Some families seemed to encounter one problem after another because the parents were so involved in Christian work. Consequently, we were concerned about failing our children in some way. We discussed this issue many times.

Then one day, I asked a respected pastor's advice. "Do you think I am making a mistake by being so involved in Bill's ministry?"

He wisely answered, "Vonette, those children belong to God and will turn out the way He directs. As long as you obey Him, you can trust Him with your sons."

Then I began to notice how many lay people have similar problems. I realized that a parent's position in life matters less than his commitment to his children and to his heavenly Father.

We're not saying that your actions will not influence your children. The opposite is true. But when you commit yourself to the Lord and to your partner, and you obey scriptural commands in parenting, you can be at peace that whatever happens in your family is part of God's plan.

Fourth, *give your children adequate attention.* This means investing time on a daily basis to encourage them, instruct them, listen to them, and share special moments with them.

There have been many occasions when, because of unexpected emergencies, we have had to be flexible as a family. Bill could easily have postponed his mountain trip with Brad and Zac to meet with the football coach. However, he felt the need to be with our sons. So he visited with the coach for a few minutes, then tactfully explained—in the presence of Brad and Zac—his prior commitment to them and set off to enjoy a day in the mountain snow with his two favorite guys. And what a time they had!

How long has it been since you put down the newspaper or turned off the TV and sat down face to face to share with your children? Have you praised them recently for good behavior or complimented them for a task well done? Can they count on you to be there for them when they have a problem?

Just being "on deck" for your children means a lot. When our boys were young, for example, Bill would come home for dinner even though his work wasn't finished. He would often wrestle with them or engage in fun games until they went to bed, then go back to the office and complete his work. Not only did he feel refreshed after such a wonderful break, but he also shared the best part of our sons' day. He got to enjoy a meal with us and then tuck them into bed.

Even when he was traveling the world, Bill always made himself available to the boys and me. I knew he would catch the next plane home if we needed him.

Fifth, *use godly principles in discipline.* Like every other family, we had problems with discipline. We did not rear two boys who reached sainthood before the age of five. When they were young, Bill often found it necessary to spank them or correct them in other ways. But we tried to follow three rules in the process:

1. We tried never to discipline the boys when we were angry. The purpose of discipline is not to vent wrath, but to correct and instruct. Anger provokes children and teaches them to fear. We asked the Lord to help us correct our children in a biblical way. Early on we explained to our sons that God disciplines us when we are disobedient because He loves us (Proverbs 3:11,12). We tried to reinforce this with the boys until they understood why they had to be corrected.

2. We apologized for mistakes. When Zac was a junior in high school, he had an appointment with his orthodontist. Before he left for school in the morning, I reminded him, "Don't forget your retainer. The dentist has to check it."

That afternoon I picked him up at school to take him to the doctor. On the way, I asked, "You brought your retainer, didn't you?"

"Oh, Mother, I forgot," he groaned.

"Where is it?"

"At home."

I felt irritated. "I reminded you to take it this morning. Now we don't have time to run home to pick it up." My anger mounted. "You could have called me. But no, you didn't even *think* about the trouble you've caused." Zac didn't respond and silence prevailed as I continued to fume to myself.

Suddenly, it seemed as if God pointed a finger at me. "You are certainly not modeling a good example as a mother." Mentally I replayed the words I had spoken to Zac.

"I'm sorry," I sighed to him. "I've been hard on you. I shouldn't have become angry. When I tried to help you learn to be more responsible, I lost my temper."

Zac smiled. "That's okay." A few minutes later he said softly, "I'm sorry about forgetting. I'll try to do better next time."

My apology brought out the best in Zac and helped him to see that parents can admit when they are wrong. When I stopped the car at the orthodontist's office, he ran to the other side to open my door. He opened the door to the office and made sure I had a place to sit. He even picked out a magazine for me to read.

3. *We tried to follow through once we set rules.* Bill and I discovered this wasn't easy to do.

When Brad was two years old, for example, he began to assert his independence. He deliberately spilled his milk on the floor. I spanked him. In anger, he threw a package of napkins into the milk.

"Brad, pick them up," I said firmly.

He didn't budge.

"If you don't, I'll have to spank you again."

He shook his head. I picked up a small paddle and used it once. He still refused to obey. Another swat, followed by continued stubbornness.

Bill and I were in a difficult position. Our son was determined to assert his will. We could have given in, picked up the napkins and soothed, "Okay, but next time..."

It was quite a scene. Brad was sobbing, then Bill and I were crying. This went on for several minutes. Finally, I took his hand and made him bend down to pick up the napkins.

Then we both hugged him and told him that we loved him. We tried to explain why we insisted that he obey. At two years of age he probably didn't understand all that we told him. But we weren't disciplining for the moment; we were looking to the years ahead and adulthood.

Parental authority should never be used for your own convenience, but for the good of your children. Help them understand clearly what you expect of them. And make sure your rules and standards provide a proper atmosphere for their development.

Sixth, *provide a stable home environment*. As Christian parents, we have a serious responsibility to provide as stable a home environment as possible.

One of the best ways to accomplish this is to model Christ-like love. Since children are prone to emulate our perceptions, prejudices, and preferences, we need to look at the way we treat them, examine our actions toward them and others, and check our attitude toward the world.

Setting limits adds stability to a home environment as well. A survey among the most well-adjusted children in a school found that all the children had three things in common: 1) their parents loved each other; 2) the children knew they were wanted and loved; and 3) discipline was consistent. According to the survey, children who know their boundaries feel secure.

As your children grow older, expand their boundaries to give them room for growth and maturity. Explain why you curtail certain activities, especially during adolescence. This helps them see that the rules are for their benefit, not yours.

Bill

Vonette and I would hate to think of the kind of people we might be today without the lessons we learned as parents. By following the guidelines we have discussed, you too can manage the stress of children and keep your marriage vibrant. Through difficulties and pressure, you can build eternal values into your children that will continue long after you are gone. These will be passed on to your children's children for generations.

Hanging Tough

Each of us have unavoidable and unexpected adversities that disrupt our lives, strain our relationships, and leave us with haunting memories. Some crises last a few hours; others go on for years. Yet each gives us the breathless sense of being out of control.

How do we respond to traumatic events? Must we sit quietly and watch stressful circumstances tear our family apart? Or do we use them to enrich our marriage?

Crises come in many forms and they affect families differently. Knowing how to cope can mean the difference between letting a catastrophe cripple your family and growing through your difficulties.

Let me share three principles that will help you manage the devastating events in your life and keep your marriage vibrant during rough times:

First, *maintain a vital spiritual relationship.* Do you view a crisis as a time of danger and heartache? Or do you see it as an opportunity to expand your faith and become all that God has planned for you to be? Crisis stimulates spiritual growth. In facing adversity, we need an eternal perspective; we need to see it from God's viewpoint.

It was during "KC '83" that I experienced one of my greatest personal losses. In 1983 Campus Crusade held a student Christmas conference in Kansas City. Vonette and I gathered with almost 20,000 staff and college students for an exciting week of training in discipleship and evangelism.

Billy Graham was our featured speaker. President Reagan had graciously made a videotape addressing the students saying generous things about us and Campus Crusade for Christ. I planned to share the tape and highlights from the conference with my darling, saintly mother in Coweta, Oklahoma, only a short distance away, as soon as the conference ended. I knew she would love it.

Before the meetings began, I held a press conference. As I made my final remarks to the reporters, someone handed me a note. My older sister who lived near Mother in Oklahoma was on the telephone.

Her voice quivered. "Bill, Mother just passed away. This afternoon as we were talking on the telephone, she told me that she was tired and wanted to take a nap before lunch. Apparently she went to be with the Lord while she was asleep."

Only a few minutes had passed after their conversation because a nurse found Mother when she brought her lunch.

I was devastated. Although my mother was 93 years old and was eager to see her precious Savior, I would miss her terribly. I would have seen her in just a few days, but now she was gone.

Immediately, I went to my hotel room to pray. I was scheduled to give the keynote address to this great gathering of enthusiastic students that evening. But how could I?

Where would I find the strength, courage, and calmness I needed?

While on my knees, the Lord reminded me that because of His death for my sins and His resurrection and indwelling presence in my life, He would infuse me with His strength and enable me to give the message. So I gave the address that night. I chose to go on in the strength and peace the Lord would provide in spite of my grief. God blessed me with what could well have been one of my most powerful messages.

> *God will bring order out of chaos and turn tragedy into triumph when you remain faithful to Him.*

If you are in the midst of a personal crisis, Vonette and I urge you not to make hasty decisions or consider your situation hopeless. Instead, put your trust in your loving heavenly Father to bring good out of the situation. He is full of compassion and mercy and will not abandon you. As with Job, God will bring order out of chaos and turn tragedy into triumph when you remain faithful to Him, trusting, praising, and thanking Him during your suffering.

Second, *pull together*. The entire family suffers when just one member goes through a crisis. Pulling together as marriage partners is absolutely essential if we are to keep our family from splintering while under pressure.

We must not underestimate the value of family support during times of crisis. Each person has a unique contribution toward keeping the family unit healthy and caring during hard times. Wives most often shine at preserving unity, at building esteem, and at encouraging optimism and cooperation between family members. Many times husbands are best at controlling aggressive behavior and helping maintain rules and procedures that enable the family to function. Every member of the family has his or her own strengths to bring to the troubled family. Even the youngest child can add laughter and sparkle to a saddened household.

Third, *get help.* Sometimes a crisis is so devastating, a family doesn't know how to rebuild. In this situation, spouses need to reach outside the family circle for counsel and support.

Be open with your Christian friends about your problems and heartaches. Shared spiritual commitment can bolster sagging spirits and help mend torn emotions.

I am convinced that most of our problems can be resolved by saturating our minds with the Word of God, claiming His promises, and drawing from the supernatural resources of the indwelling, risen Christ through the Holy Spirit. But sometimes only Spirit-directed Christian psychologists or pastors trained in biblical counseling can unravel the tangle of emotions wrapped around a family in crisis.

Vonette and I have seen the fruits of standing firm when life's storms rocked our frail family boat. We have watched our gracious Lord calm the winds in some situations and stand beside us to ride out the waves in others. Always, He has been faithful. Trust Him. Let Him be your source of strength.

ↀ

For Reflection, Discussion, and Action

1. In what area is your family experiencing stress today? How will you deal with the stress?

2. Think about your relationship with your spouse. Are you giving your partner top priority as you deal with the stress of parenting? If not, what steps can you take toward this goal?

3. Consistency in training and discipline of children is often difficult to maintain. How can biblical principles for raising children help you to be more consistent?

4. How can you "hang tough" through a family crisis? Give an example of how you have applied this to your relationship.

5. Think of a crisis that your family has experienced recently. How did you cope?

6. Share practical ways in which couples can "pull together" and keep their relationship vibrant during extended periods of family stress.

7. Are you building a truly godly home for your family? What specific steps can you take to move toward this goal?

Chapter 6

Women Can Make a Difference

A Word to Women From Vonette

❧

Y EARS AGO, the move of our international headquarters to Arrowhead Springs took me away from an active campus ministry at UCLA, away from our church—the First Presbyterian Church of Hollywood—where we were established and involved, and away from long-time friends.

At first, I assisted in establishing the conference center, aided in beginning the lay ministry, and helped write Crusade training materials. All of this was exciting and I loved being involved with Bill, though it was different from what we had known on the campus.

As the ministry grew, God brought us qualified people who were able to assume responsibility for some of the areas in which I had been involved.

Although I loved being at home more and having time of my own to manage, I found myself frustrated at times by a lack of challenge. I didn't feel as productive and person- ally involved in Bill's activities as I had once been.

In conversations with Bill, I would often express my concern and ask what he thought I should do.

One day he put his arms around me tenderly and said, "Honey, if you can just keep our home running smoothly while our sons are young, you will be of the most help to me. I understand there are many other things you could be doing. But right now the boys and I need you in our home."

Although Bill and the children occupied the highest place in my life after the Lord, my diminished involve- ment in the ministry still threatened my sense of signifi- cance. Even as I struggled with the transition, I realized that having committed my life to Christ, knowing Bill loved me, knowing I was contributing to our personal and ministry goals, was enough. I joyfully decided to fit in where Bill needed me, a decision I have never regretted.

My willingness to fit in where most needed for our family's sake enabled Bill to function more effectively as president of our rapidly expanding organization and al- lowed me to enjoy the fuller privileges of motherhood and homemaking. I began to pour my energies more into our children's activities, the PTA, and our church.

Undoubtedly every career woman faces the temptation to put her family in second place. I could have easily done that. The question we all ask is, "How can I make a maximum long-range contribution to making the world a better place in which to live for the glory of God?" or in my case, "How do we build a secure, loving home in a pull- apart world?"

Making a Difference

Some time ago I spoke at a New England area conference for female students from Smith, Radcliff, Mount Holyoke, MIT, Yale, Harvard, Dartmouth, Brown, and other universities. The message I shared with them was that the influence and impact of their lives and the lives of other women like them will determine what life will be like in the 21st century.

"Today's woman," writes Elizabeth Skoglund, a contemporary author, "has potential for growth, opportunity for equality, and a choice of roles. She can compete with pride in the marketplace, and she can, with equal dignity, stay at home and raise children. Or, she can do both. Above all, she can still be a woman, no matter what her role."

Proverbs 31 describes one model of Christian womanhood. I appreciate the way one unidentified writer has paraphrased her characteristics (verses 11–27):

- She faithfully satisfies and supports her husband, a respected leader in the community.
- She provides food and beautiful clothing for her household.
- She directs and manages the household servants.
- She invests in real estate and engages in commercial agriculture, financed by her own earnings.
- She trades for profit and does charitable work.
- She teaches wisely, diligently cares for her children, and administrates the affairs of her household.

What a woman!

Now before you panic, let me say that God doesn't want you to run a ten-ring circus. Nor does he require you to pursue the lifestyle of the Proverbs woman. She is an example of what God enables a woman to be—if she so chooses.

God does not view the fair sex as second-rate human beings but as unique individuals with almost unlimited capabilities. So the question is not, "Can I influence my world as a Christian?" but rather, "What kind of influence am I going to have?" As women, we *will* have an influence—and knowing that will determine the choices we make. We must make sure that our lives serve as positive, constructive, and eternal examples.

I believe the most rewarding, sustaining lifestyle is one rooted in a personal, trusting relationship with Jesus Christ, characterized by obedience to the way of life He desires. We experience this as we place the full weight of our identity not on what we are, but on the One who will never change.

Women significantly determine the moral standards of a nation. Writing of the United States in the early 1800s, De Tocqueville said in *Democracy in America*, "Now as I come to the end of this book in which I have recorded so many considerable achievements of the Americans, if anyone asks me what I think was the chief cause of the extraordinary prosperity and the growing power of this nation, I should answer that it is due to the superiority of her women."

This is even more true today, and consequently, we women have an awesome responsibility to use our talents and gifts to make a difference in our homes, in our communities, and in our nation.

Building a Godly Home

The Proverbs 31 woman, however, achieves her greatest influence in her home. Her first priority is to meet the needs of her loved ones. Although she works outside the home, she gives her foremost attention to the needs of her husband and children. She is a marvelous, realistic model of how we, too, can build a godly home in the midst of a pull-apart world. Here are three key principles that she exemplifies:

First, *fear God.* "A woman who fears and reverences God shall be greatly praised" (Proverbs 31:30, TLB).

Usually the woman sets the atmosphere and pace in the home. She may establish either a calm, loving mood or a hectic, disagreeable one. If she neglects her spiritual walk, her family suffers. But if she depends on the Holy Spirit, she can create a place where everyone feels comfortable and secure.

Let me encourage you to feast on the Word of God daily to refresh your spirit and keep your moods gentle and loving. Fill your home with the sound of recorded Scripture, Christian songs, and hymns. This will help you establish an environment in which you can settle squabbles, discipline children, and soothe hurt feelings with the mercy and justice that only God can give you.

Many men will not compete for spiritual headship and will bow out if their wives insist on taking the spiritual leadership role. If your husband accepts his God-given role as the priest and servant-leader of his home, encourage his efforts and help him gain confidence in his leadership.

But what happens if your husband's job frequently takes him away from home? Or if he neglects or refuses to serve as the priest in your family? Should you assume the spiritual leadership?

Yes. Accept the responsibility as if he had delegated it to you. Gently and lovingly encourage him in his relationship with God. More important, pray constantly for him and trust the Lord to enable him to accept his God-given responsibility in the home.

Keep in mind that one purpose of the home is to rear children in the fear of the Lord in order to help them develop character, integrity, and purpose. This will enable them to take their God-given place on the world scene as responsible and accountable citizens and as leaders who will help to build a better world.

Second, *make your home a priority.* "She watches carefully all that goes on throughout her household, and is never lazy" (Proverbs 31:27, TLB).

> *No institution is more important than the home. Through our families we build the church and our nation.*
>
> ❧

No institution is more important than the home. An atmosphere of love, loyalty, and caring can best be maintained within the family circle. Self-esteem and acceptance flourish like well-watered plants. Through our families we build the church and our nation.

Yet this world often tells us that wifely duties rank below many other activities. The secular community wants us to believe that cooking, cleaning, wiping runny noses, and changing diapers do not have the dressing of success.

These pressures are why a wife must make sure her home is top priority. I regard my responsibilities as wife and mother a privilege and the highest calling.

The daughter of our dear friend Mrs. Louis Evans, Sr. told me a story about her mother. When she was a young girl, she came home to find her mother sitting on the back steps, head in her hands, exhausted. The daughter noticed a long line of freshly-beaten rugs on the clothesline.

"Oh, Mother," she lamented as she sat beside her, "I am so sorry you have to work so hard. You could have been a great musician or a wonderful teacher. But here you are a housewife."

At her words, Mrs. Evans picked herself up proudly. "My dear, I am *not* the wife of a house. I am building a home. And that takes a lot of beating of rugs, washing dishes, and caring for children."

Many times over the years, the pulls of the outside world threatened to distort my focus. I have had to reassess my priorities continually. Physical arrangements sometimes posed a special challenge. When will I clean my house? Do I have time for the laundry? Or: Am I so wrapped up in minor housekeeping details that I'm neglecting my family's emotional needs? Or opportunities to minister to others?

All these concerns required constant evaluation.

A dedicated wife, I learned, commits herself daily to the task of building a godly home. She cannot afford to let others shoulder her responsibility. That doesn't mean that she can't get support from outside the home. But she sees to the welfare of each member personally.

Third, *reach out to others through your home.* "She sews for the poor, and generously helps those in need" (Proverbs 31:19,20, TLB).

Bill's mother, Mary Lee, was a modern example of the Proverbs 31 woman. She was a well-educated, fine-fibered person, a former teacher who enjoyed classical literature and cherished her Bible. She married a cattle rancher and gave birth to eight children. Although life on the ranch was not easy in rural America at that time, she lived a godly life before her family and friends and never complained or criticized another person. She made her home a haven for the family and was always available to care for neighbors in need. Her home was so popular that she often did not know how many would be present for a meal. Many watermelon and ice cream socials attracted friends from near and far.

When anyone in the community brought up the subject of the most godly person they knew, Mrs. Bright's name usually came up first. And her influence is still felt around the world through her family.

I encourage you to enlist your family's creativity to make your home a center for evangelism and caring. Entertain non-Christian friends, or lead an evangelistic coffee for women. Build friendships with neighbors and share Jesus Christ with them.

Why not celebrate Christmas with a birthday party for Jesus and invite your children's playmates? Bible clubs for children in your backyard present an excellent opportunity as well.

Plan a picnic with a non-Christian family. Encourage your husband and children to pray for each guest ahead of time. Help your family care for the needs of your visitors and share their testimonies with someone during the outing.

Helping Your Husband Succeed as a Leader

The Proverbs 31 woman helped her husband succeed (Proverbs 31:11,12). He trusted her because of her unselfish attitudes and actions. Would you like to know how to encourage your husband to reach his full potential, despite the pressures of his hectic life? Let me give you four suggestions:

First, *intercede for him*. Bringing your husband's needs and stresses before the Lord is the greatest service you can do for him.

I keep a prayer diary. Of course, Bill heads the top of the list. I record specific prayer requests, asking the Lord to give him discernment in the decisions he must make. I pray for his spiritual walk, his physical health, and the influence that others have on him and that he has on those around him.

Often, he will mention a situation of concern. Sometimes he asks me to pray for him at a certain time of the day. I bring these matters to the Lord, then ask later about the results.

Whatever method you use to pray for your husband, be consistent and faithful. Thank the Lord for the growth and maturity you see in his life, and for the contribution he makes to you and your home.

Second, *support his leadership*. There can be only one head in a marriage relationship. God ordained that position for the husband. Napoleon said he would rather have one weak commander than two strong ones who were constantly competing. There should never be any strife for supremacy in the marriage partnership. The apostle Paul writes:

Wives, submit to your husbands as to the Lord. For the husband is the head of the wife as Christ is the head of the church...Now as the church submits to Christ, so also wives should submit to their husbands in everything (Ephesians 5:22–24, NIV).

The apostle gives this direction after first admonishing, "Submit to one another out of reverence for Christ" (verse

21). Paul leaves no doubt, however, as to who should have the final authority. And he makes it clear that the wife should voluntarily follow her husband's leadership in all areas. That does not mean she blindly follows or has no input to where that leadership will lead. The wise husband who loves his wife "as Christ also loved the church" will consult her and work toward agreement.

From the beginning of our marriage, I found it easy to support and promote my husband because he knew where he was going. He had vision. He had courage. He had faith. And he was willing to take risks for the Lord. I was eager to make a contribution to his life and ministry. As a result, I looked for ways in which I could complement and be an encouragement to him. I sought his advice and his direction, checking to make sure I was doing what he needed most.

The apostle Peter describes a wife's submission to her husband as beautiful (1 Peter 3:5, NIV). Proverbs 31:11,12 praises the noble wife because she is one who richly satisfies her husband's needs. She supplies what no one else can.

Some women believe that this role as a homemaker is demeaning and makes her inferior and less significant. But Jesus explained:

> Whoever wants to become great among you must be your servant, and whoever wants to be first must be your slave—just as the Son of Man did not come to be served, but to serve, and to give his life as a ransom for many (Matthew 20:26–28, NIV).

Bill often says that the three greatest influences in his life have been women: his mother, me, and Dr. Henrietta Mears. Women have the greatest opportunity as wives and mothers to fulfill that Scripture and follow our Lord's example.

One of the essential ingredients of being supportive in submission is adapting. We need to fit in with our husbands' plans and schedules. Rather than trying to make our husbands conform to us, we should help maximize their potential, enabling them to be all they possibly can be.

Wives, if we don't adapt, we put a tremendous strain on our marriage. We cause our husbands either to abandon their leadership roles or to rigidly enforce rules. Our lack of conformity to God's order in the family weakens our partnership.

Consider submission a trust from God. Remember that supporting your husband is obedience to your heavenly Father also.

Third, *respect him.* Have you ever watched a wife who outwardly submits to her husband but inwardly holds him in contempt? She effectively destroys their marital intimacy and undermines his self-esteem.

If we understand the differences between men and women, we will recognize the importance of treating our husbands with deep respect. Generally, women need love and security for fulfillment while men seek after significance and recognition. Respect is one way a husband achieves significance.

You may say, "I cannot respect my husband."

Then praise and affirm him in the areas in which he excels. Help him with his weaknesses in a non-threatening, confidential manner. Support him in what he believes God has called him to do.

When Bill stepped out in faith to buy Arrowhead Springs, many people believed he was making a grave mistake. One friend, one of our major financial supporters, strongly opposed our purchasing Arrowhead and kept expecting the project to fail. When Bill didn't agree with him, the friend warned, "If you buy this property, I won't give any more money to the ministry."

He was faithful to his word.

But he took me aside one day. "Don't worry, Vonette," he said calmly. "I've set aside a large sum of money to take care of you and Bill and the ministry when this project falls through and Bill falls flat on his face."

Although my faith was shaky, I supported my husband and assured our friend, "God will supply our needs."

Of course, the Lord did meet our needs day by day, month by month, until the miracle of Arrowhead Springs was complete and our final payment was made. Through the years since the purchase of Arrowhead Springs in 1962, hundreds of thousands of people from all over the world have received training in discipleship and evangelism there.

In the meantime, I learned a valuable lesson. Although in private I may question or disagree with Bill, publicly I always support him when he believes God is leading him to undertake a special project. I choose to put aside our differences to work beside him. That is one way I can show how much I respect and believe in him.

Be sensitive to how you can increase your husband's stature among his friends and co-workers. When he feels discouraged, help him stick to the course he has set. Don't make mountains out of molehills if he displays poor judgment.

Fourth, *listen to him*. Men need their wives to listen to them.

A few years ago, I began doing a lot of needlepoint. After completing four or five pieces, I started on a large project. As I was finishing, Bill asked, "You aren't going to do *more* needlepoint, are you?"

"Why would you say that?" I asked, surprised.

"It seems to me that you could be doing something far more important with your time."

His comment made me analyze the situation. At every opportunity, I would concentrate on my needlepoint, usually on an airplane. As I sewed, I would listen to a tape and get lost in my thoughts while Bill read different books. We weren't talking as much. Soon after I completed that project, I put away my sewing and began listening to him and he to me.

Involved as I am, I have to make time to listen. No matter what the demands of my work, when Bill needs my attention, he comes first. I may have to ask him to delay our conversation until later, but I honor his request.

Take the time to let your husband share what is on his mind and heart. He may express his thoughts factually rather than emotionally, but give him an opportunity to tell you about his failures and discouragements without criticism. Express your admiration for his successes. Build his trust by keeping his confidences. It may be necessary to set specific times to talk so you can give him your undivided attention.

Building Bridges Between Family and Career

One of the major challenges faced by today's family is achieving balance. We *do* live in a pull-apart world where the demands of the work environment often destroy the unity in the home. But you can minimize the effects of this pressure by maintaining a positive attitude toward your career, enlisting the cooperation of your family, and inviting your family to participate when decisions must be made.

To keep a positive attitude toward the demands of your career, remind yourself of the fulfillment and rewards of your work.

Involve your family in your professional life. Describe your work duties and talk about the people you see at your office. Take your husband and children on a tour of the workplace.

Enlist the cooperation of your family by inviting them to share in the daily chores. The scrambled eggs may taste rubbery when your teenage son cooks them, but learn to appreciate his efforts anyway.

If your daughter misses more spots than she cleans when washing the floor, use the opportunity to teach her how to do a thorough job. Be willing to lower your standards a little when your preschooler straightens his room.

Avoid criticism. Many wives sabotage their efforts to gain cooperation by never being satisfied with the results. Instead, praise your husband and children when they help.

Gently correct your children when they intentionally do an unsatisfactory job. Recognize the difference between laziness and a lack of maturity to handle the responsibility. Expecting more of a child than he is mature enough to accomplish will only frustrate him.

Family participation in decision making is a vital span on the bridge between family and career. Have you ever noticed how much harder a person works if he is involved in the decisions that are made? Or how he drags his feet if someone imposes a job on him? Sometimes women make important decisions that affect their families without discussing the issues with the family.

If you are planning a party in your home, for example, discuss your plans with the whole family—first. You can imagine how much more enthusiastically everyone would respond.

Consider your family a team. Encourage them to use their gifts, talents, and personalities to help ease the pressure for you of too little time and too many jobs. Of course, there still will be moments when you have to insist firmly that your family help. But with your positive encouragement, they will more likely feel that their contributions to family life are valuable and desired.

I encourage you to make your home the center of your attention, even though you live a busy life. Use your talents to create a nest where each person can stretch and grow in a cradle of security. The result will be a unified group that can more effectively manage the stresses of living in a fast-paced world.

Don't be discouraged if you can't make the change all at once. Change requires time, commitment, and maturity. But in this world of turmoil, the rewards for providing a stable, loving, Christ-centered home cannot be equaled.

With time, we can become more like the godly woman of Proverbs 31 who is a woman of "strength and dignity" (Proverbs 31:25). And the results of our dignity?

Her children stand and bless her; so does her husband. He praises her with these words: "There are many fine women in the world, but you are the best of them all!" (Proverbs 31:28,29, TLB).

Who could ask for higher praise and satisfaction in building a home in a pull-apart world?

৶

For Reflection, Discussion, and Action

1. List several women who have influenced your life for good. How did their examples inspire you?

2. How can you make your home a priority and still reach out to others? Implement at least one of these ideas this week.

3. In what ways are you helping your husband succeed as a leader? What additional things can you do to strengthen his potential as a leader?

Chapter 7

Radical Lover— Intimate Leader

A Word to Men From Bill

ða

A JAPANESE magazine has a picture of a butterfly on one of its pages. Its wings are a dull gray until the picture is warmed by one's hand. The touch causes the special inks in the printing to react, and the butterfly is transformed into a rainbow of color.

Throughout this book, Vonette and I have shared many principles that will help you transform your marriage and home into a rainbow of beauty. At this point you may wonder, "Where do I begin?"

Everything we have said hinges upon one basic premise in God's Word:

Husbands, love your wives, just as Christ also loved the church and gave Himself up for her (Ephesians 5:25).

Radical Love

What does it mean to love your wife as Christ loved the church? Why is this love so crucial?

Every Christian husband knows he should love his wife. But few really understand that it takes a radical kind of love to enjoy a truly healthy, happy marriage.

Loving as Christ loves *is* radical. Picture it this way: Radical love is a finely cut diamond with many sparkling facets. Let's consider four of these facets for a moment.

First, *radical love is sacrificial.* Unlike the Hollywood image of love that is based on lust and selfishness, Christ's love is rooted in selflessness and sacrifice. The apostle Paul's words to the Ephesians provide the key to this principle: Christ *gave himself up* for the church. Sacrificial love cost our Savior His life—on the cross.

Likewise, Christ's love calls upon us to make sacrifices, to yield our rights and preferences for the sake of our wives, to lay aside our personal desires and ambitions for those of our spouses, to love sincerely and purely, with cordial and ardent affection, to cherish without reservation regardless of our partners' imperfections and failures.

We cannot love sacrificially in our own strength. By nature, we are jealous, envious, and boastful. We are proud, haughty, selfish, and rude, and we demand our own way. But God puts His love into our hearts by the Holy Spirit the moment we receive Jesus Christ into our lives.

How long has it been since you showed sacrificial love to your wife? Take a moment, right now, to reflect on this question. Think of ways you can "give yourself up" to your wife. Make a list. Then ask God by faith to help you love her sacrificially as Christ loves the church.

Second, *radical love takes the initiative.* Christ's sacrificial love can take a strife-torn marriage and transform it into a beautiful, rich relationship. Perhaps you are thinking, "But you don't know *my* wife. She's impossible! When she changes her attitude, I'll change mine!"

Radical love, however, is aggressive. It takes the initiative. It follows God's precept of "first love" (1 John 4:19). It reaches out in reconciliation when she is least deserving.

With the purest and deepest kind of love, our Lord modeled this principle. He took the initiative to reconcile us while we were yet in sin. Paul said that God showed his great love for us by sending Christ to die for us while we were still sinners (Romans 5:6–8).

The Greek word used in the Scriptures to describe this love is *agape*. It is expressed not through mere emotions, but as an act of one's will. We must not wait to *feel* loving before taking the initiative. We must choose to love by *faith*.[1]

When Jesus sacrificed Himself on the cross for our sins, He did so by faith that we would respond to His redeeming love. He didn't wait until we were good; He loved first. This is what our Lord's "first love" principle means.

If you and your wife are experiencing conflict, I encourage you to begin loving her by faith. Take the first step in reconciliation. Ask the Holy Spirit to fill you with His power and Christ's radical love. Then pray for her. Talk to her. Show concern for her needs. And watch God work through you to calm the storm.

Third, *radical love is considerate.* Many couples suffer needless turmoil because the husband is inconsiderate of his wife. Vonette and I are no exception.

Vonette is strong and shares her opinions freely, and I always know where she stands on issues. I like her that way. Her sensitivities and abilities complement mine, and in many instances she has helped me see how to better

---

[1] For more information on this principle, see my booklet entitled *How You Can Love by Faith* (NewLife Publications).

solve a problem. But in the early years of our marriage, I
didn't always appreciate her way of thinking.

If she disagreed with a decision I had made, I saw her
as a deterrent to my plans and felt threatened. I had made
up my mind and that was that! And instead of discussing
the problem, I often walked out of the house.

The apostle Peter admonishes, "Husbands...be considerate as you live with your wives, and treat them with
respect as the weaker partner and as heirs with you of the
gracious gift of life, so that nothing will hinder your
prayers" (1 Peter 3:7, NIV).

Being considerate, I have discovered, means treating
Vonette with respect and valuing her opinions. Over the
years, I have learned to talk about our differences and be
more understanding of her needs and her temperament. I
have realized that the Lord often speaks through her, so
when we disagree I listen to her viewpoint.

And I no longer head for the nearest door.

Sometimes it's the little things that count most in being
considerate of our wives. Like coming home from the
office on time when Vonette has taken precious moments
to prepare me a delicious meal.

Then there's picking up after myself. The last thing
Vonette wants to do is clean up my mess at home after she's
put in a hard day at the office or just before guests arrive.

Going shopping with your wife also shows consideration.

One evening when I was almost buried behind a stack
of "urgent" reading materials and dictations, Vonette
needed to go to the grocery store.

"Do you have time to go with me?" she asked.

Grocery shopping wasn't exactly what I had in mind for
my evening. But I don't like Vonette going out alone after
dark.

I laughed. "It'll be a sacrifice and a tremendous challenge to my future, but I will."

I'm like a kid in a candy store when it comes to grocery shopping. As we strolled the aisles, I kept throwing items into our cart. I spotted all kinds of bargains—and diet food. I even grabbed a can opener on sale.

By the time we reached the check-out counter, we looked like a couple buying groceries for a huge family. Our bill was considerably higher than when Vonette shops alone.

But she loves it when I go with her. Shopping turns into a safari, stalking groceries in a forest of shelves. And we come home with a car full of bagged prey.

Taking interest in projects around the house is another way to be considerate.

Some years ago, we decided to redecorate our house. The carpet had grown threadbare and the sofas needed recovering. We had entertained approximately 60,000 guests for dinners, luncheons, and receptions since the house had last been decorated. And because of limited funds, we had put off redecorating for a long time.

One day a staff member said very kindly, "Bill, your home is the 'White House' of this ministry. If you don't have the money to redecorate it, I will." I got the message.

Together we began making our selections of decor and color. We readily agreed on most of our choices, but the living room was not pulling together.

I like blue. If I had my way, it would be the dominant color throughout the house, particularly in the living room. But Vonette wasn't excited about my choice so we kept working at our selection until we both were happy.

She sought the advice of a decorator friend, who suggested a color scheme of coral with light blue accents. Vonette was sure I would never accept that.

Of course, I try to impress her that my taste in decorating is superior to hers! But actually her preference usually is best. I took one look at the decorator's suggestion and exclaimed, "That's it! Vonette looks great in coral. Let's wrap the living room around her."

The coral color pulled the blue decor together beautifully and we were both happy with the result.

I'm sure you can think of many other ways to be considerate. Take a few moments right now to jot down your ideas. Be creative. Ask God to help you. Showing consideration to your wife, even the smallest amount, will go a long way toward reducing the tensions in your marriage.

Fourth, *radical love encourages development.* A considerate husband will always encourage his wife to develop spiritually, personally, socially, and vocationally.

On one occasion, a young man expressed his concern that many single women who are involved in ministry are not interested in marriage for fear they will lose their significance in ministry.

I replied, "I don't blame them. If a man desires a wife to be only his housekeeper, laundress, and cook, what woman would want to sacrifice serving the Lord in a significant ministry for such an unrewarding role?"

A man who wishes to make a woman his partner will realize that they can achieve more together than either could separately. A woman will respond to partnership and look upon that kind of relationship as a significant ministry and lifestyle.

Many of us were reared to be "macho men." A husband and father was the lord of his kingdom and he expected his wife and children to bow to his every demand. Quite a contrast to the example of our dear Lord as described in Philippians:

Your attitude should be the kind that was shown us by Jesus Christ, who, though he was God, did not demand and cling to his rights as God, but laid aside his mighty power and glory, taking the disguise of a slave and becoming like men. And he humbled himself even further, going so far as actually to die a criminal's death on a cross (Philippians 2:5–8, TLB).

The only way to love as Christ did is to walk in the power of the Holy Spirit moment by moment as He did. Only He can enable you to have that supernatural, unconditional, unshakable love for your wife.

I encourage you to lay aside your personal desires and ambitions to meet her needs as Christ did for us. Love without reservation or expecting anything in return. Pour your life into hers. Be sensitive to her. Consult her and respect her judgment. Keep her informed on the issues that concern you.

Intimate Leader

Why is loving our wives as Christ loved the church so crucial? Because our Lord commands it and because out of radical love emerges intimate leadership.

> *Only Christ can enable you to have that supernatural, unconditional, unshakable love for your wife.*

Next to his relationship with the Lord, an intimate leader is one who sees ministering to his wife as his highest calling in life.

Our first priority in this calling is to model spiritual leadership. A godly husband realizes that he shows through his example how the heavenly Father relates with His children. So this man takes seriously the biblical admonition to be "head of the wife, as Christ also is the head of the church" (Ephesians 5:23).

As high priest in his home, he prepares himself for leadership through consistent Bible study and prayer. He understands his accountability before God to nurture his wife in her walk with the Lord. Following the example of our Lord, he leads her with gentleness and consideration and never finds it necessary to demand submission. His character and example inspire cooperation and trust.

He creates an environment of warmth and intimacy by sharing himself with her, by including her in the little things in his life.

Does this sound like an impossible journey? None of us can expect to achieve intimate leadership with sinless perfection. But we can rely on the power of the Holy Spirit to transform us into men of God, enabling us to love by faith.

An intimate leader also takes the lead in evangelism.

I am convinced by the examples and teachings of our Lord Jesus and the church of the New Testament that every Christian is commanded to be an aggressive witness for Christ and help fulfill the Great Commission of our Lord (Mark 16:15; Matthew 28:19). The duty of every intimate leader is to inspire his wife and children by example and deed to obey this command.

When Vonette and I moved into our home in Bel Air, California, three minutes from the UCLA campus, I was excited about how we could use it for our ministry. The first day we lived in that house, I spoke to a group of men at one of the fraternities. After the meeting, a young man followed me home for counsel and was the first to receive Christ in our house. Eventually, hundreds of students experienced their first moments of new birth within those walls.

The best place to model our passion for lost souls is at home. Ministering to others in the core of family life also teaches each member of the family how to share Christ's love and forgiveness.

Today as I write, both of our sons and their wives have surrendered their lives to Christ and are serving Him in evangelism and discipleship. Zac is a Presbyterian minister, and Brad is on our Campus staff at the University of Washington in Seattle. One of the high moments of my life was when Zac asked me to teach him how to share his faith in Christ with others.

Recently, I was deeply moved when Brad called to thank me for being a man of God. Apparently he had just read of God's promise to bless the lives of the children of godly fathers. (I am sure that includes godly mothers, too.) Brad was experiencing several unusual blessings from the Lord and wanted to express his gratitude not only to God but to me also.

Can you think of a greater encouragement than knowing your children and their children for generations will be blessed if you love God, trust His promises, and obey His commands?

Building Intimate Leadership Through Radical Love

Radical love, we have seen, finds its expression in sacrifice. It takes the initiative in reconciliation. It considers others before itself. But intimate leadership embraces yet another dimension: service.

Christ's example was clear. He came to serve. The Gospel of Mark records:

> Whoever wants to become great among you must be your servant, and whoever wants to be first must be slave of all. For even the Son of Man did not come to be served, but to serve, and to give his life as a ransom for many (Mark 10:43–45).

Our Lord's disciples had great difficulty with this precept. At the Last Supper, they argued among themselves over who would be the greatest in the kingdom of God. Jesus corrected them lovingly:

> In this world the kings and great men order their slaves around, and the slaves have no choice but to like it! But among you, the one who serves you best will be your leader (Luke 22:25,26, TLB).

Godly principles often seem paradoxical. To receive, we must give. To live, we must die. To be exalted, we must be humble. To harvest, we must sow. To lead, we must serve.

The principle of servanthood is in sharp contrast to the way many husbands see themselves.

Someone once said that husbands and wives are often like boiled potatoes sitting side by side on the same platter. What they need is a "heavenly masher" to come down and make them truly one. Unfortunately, many men *see themselves* as heavenly mashers. They rule their households as though they were iron-fisted dictators. "I'm boss here!" they declare. "And you do what I say, when I say, and how I say." These husbands violate Christ's example of servanthood, love, and leadership, and they stand in the way of the Holy Spirit's work in their home.

During the Last Supper, Jesus began to wash the disciples' feet. When He came to Peter, Peter waved Him off. "Master, You shouldn't be washing our feet like this!"

Our Lord's answer is just as relevant today. "But if I don't, you can't be my partner."

Humility, Jesus was saying, is the key to a servant's heart. Without it, we cannot be partners with Him in intimate leadership.

I love Peter's response. "Then wash my hands and head as well—not just my feet" (John 13:6–9, TLB).

In other words, "Bathe me completely in Your humility, Lord. I want to be like You."

Let this be your prayer, too. Ask God to wash you thoroughly in our Lord's humility that you may be a partner with Him in leading your family. And seek to walk daily in that humility as you follow God's plan for leadership in your home.

Following God's Plan

Many families experience turmoil because the husband doesn't take his proper role as a servant leader. No husband can afford to neglect his godly responsibility. Leading your wife by our Lord's tender mercies will help you build a vibrant, exciting, harmonious relationship.

Remember this, if you forget everything else I have written: *You, more than your wife, are responsible for a healthy, happy marriage.* Women are by nature responders. Follow the counsel of this chapter, and you will discover that you will have a new wife. She will respond to your practical, creative ways of demonstrating your love.

Your marriage can be a happy or miserable experience. That decision is largely up to you.

I strongly urge you to keep your leadership on track. And to take the necessary steps to fulfill your God-given role as a radical lover and intimate leader.

❧

For Reflection, Discussion, and Action

1. Review the four qualities of radical love. How can you demonstrate these qualities in your relationship with your wife?

2. What does it mean to love one's wife "as Christ loved the church"? Name practical ways that you as a husband can love your wife in this manner.

3. What is the secret to building intimate leadership? How are you applying this principle in your relationship? In what ways can you improve?

Chapter 8

The World Awaits

ॐ

BECAUSE WE are both such strong personalities, it is not likely that we would be married today had we not discovered how to live Spirit-filled lives. We marvel that any couple who doesn't live for God in the power and control of the Holy Spirit can stay together in our pull-apart world.

The Lord understands the struggles we face in putting our trust in Him. He knows we cannot have faith on our own; it is a gift from Him (Ephesians 2:8). That is why He sent His Holy Spirit to help us fight our battles.

A Spirit-Filled Marriage

God also has given us many spiritual principles in His Word to help us build a Spirit-filled marriage. We share five of these truths now.

1. Be in love with the Lord. A love relationship with the Lord Jesus Christ is basic to establishing a spiritual marriage and a godly home. Jesus said, "You shall love the Lord your God with all your heart, and with all your soul, and with all your mind. This is the great and foremost commandment" (Matthew 22:37,38).

God desires our love just as we desire the love of our children. An incident that happened a number of years ago illustrates this:

One evening I was at the table studying while Vonette worked in another part of the house. Zac, who was then in his early teens, came into the room carrying half a dozen books. Without interrupting me, he set them on the table and began reading quietly.

Suddenly, I became conscious of his presence beside me. "Son, is there something I can do for you?" I asked softly.

"No, Dad. I just want to be near you."

Imagine how I felt! His words melted my heart. He could have gone a hundred places to be alone with his books. But he chose to be with me. That's how our precious Savior feels when our gratitude and love for Him make us long to be with Him.

2. Read the Word of God. If we are in love with Jesus, we will want to read His Word daily. The Bible is His love message to us, and we will want to discover how to please Him more each day. The psalmist declares:

Oh, the joys of those who...delight in doing everything God wants them to, and day and night are always meditating on his laws and thinking about ways to follow him more closely.

They are like trees along a river bank bearing luscious fruit each season without fail. Their leaves shall never wither, and all they do shall prosper (Psalm 1:1–3, TLB).

Like those trees, our spirits grow strong and healthy when we consistently read, study, memorize, and meditate on God's Word. Sharing the scriptures as a couple enables us to mature together in spiritual understanding and marital intimacy.

3. Spend time in prayer. Vonette and I have learned how important it is to take time each day to be alone with God. Our marriage, as well as our ministry, depends on it. We cannot possibly live the lives of victorious, fruitful Christians without nourishing our spiritual natures *daily* in prayer.

Vonette

Bill and I each have our private times alone with the Lord, though we also seek to enhance our relationship with each other by praying together. Whenever we are together, we begin and end each day on our knees for a brief time in prayer. Throughout the day we seek to maintain constant communication with our Lord. Many times during the day we lift our hearts in praise or silent prayer. Often we join members of our staff or other Christians in prayer.

People talk a lot about intimacy these days. How much closer can husbands and wives be than when they come united into God's presence? Through our years of praying together, we have learned to understand each other better; we care more, and we feel each other's pain and joy more fully.

My heart is especially warmed when Bill and I invite the Lord Jesus each day to walk around in our bodies, think with our minds, love with our hearts, speak with our lips; and because He came to seek and to save those who are lost, we ask Him to continue to seek and save the lost through us. In different words, that is our daily prayer.

4. Live a holy life. Bill and I have discovered that walking close to the Lord and obeying His commands help us keep "short accounts" with God. The apostle Paul urges:

As obedient children, do not be conformed to the former lusts which were yours in your ignorance, but like the Holy One who called you, be holy yourselves also in all your behavior; because it is written, "You shall be holy, for I am holy" (1 Peter 1:14–16).

How can Christians live holy lives? Through the years Bill has taught a concept he calls "Spiritual Breathing" (which I referred to briefly in Chapter 2). Like physical breathing, Spiritual Breathing is a process of exhaling the impure and inhaling the pure. It is an effective exercise in faith that enables you to experience God's love and forgiveness as a way of life.

To keep "short accounts" in your spiritual life and in your marriage, you can breathe spiritually the moment the Holy Spirit convicts you of a sin or a shortcoming.

First, "exhale" by confessing that sin to God, for the Bible says, "If we confess our sins, He is faithful and just to forgive us our sins and to cleanse us from all unrighteousness" (1 John 1:9, NKJ).

Confession in its original sense means to agree with God. Basically, there are three ways to agree with God: 1) that whatever you do that grieves the Holy Spirit is sin—pride, jealousy, lust, critical spirit; 2) that Christ has paid the penalty by dying on the cross and shedding His blood for your sins; and 3) that you repent—as an act of your will, you agree to change your attitude toward your acts of disobedience, which results in a change of action. You begin to obey God instead of disobeying Him. One cannot be a victorious Christian and experience a meaningful marriage relationship if he has unconfessed sin in his life. So, "exhale" the impure.

Next, "inhale" by receiving God's forgiveness and cleansing and by appropriating the fullness of the Holy Spirit in your life by faith.

God *commands* Christians to be filled with the Holy Spirit as a way of life (Ephesians 5:18). He *promises* to hear and answer all of our prayers that are consistent with His will (1 John 5:14,15). Therefore, we can claim His fullness as an act of the will by faith, based on His holy, inspired Word.

If done with a genuine desire to please God and achieve victory over sin in your life, Spiritual Breathing is all it takes to make things right between you and your heavenly Father. And it will enable the Holy Spirit to bless your marriage.

5. Apply the Throne Check. Through the years, Bill and I have used the Throne Check to test our attitudes and actions. When one of us catches himself or another member of the family doing something that doesn't please God, we gently ask the question, "Who's on the throne?"

The Throne Check provides the theological basis for relationships in our family. It reminds us of our need to have our Lord Jesus Christ in control of our lives at all times. This simple practice helps us to see that the person we feel is in the wrong is not the problem. The issue to consider is who is in control, the flesh or the Spirit? The Throne Check has enabled us to resolve many difficulties that could have erupted into major conflict.

We may not wish to admit it, but the desire for dominance plays a large role in all of our lives. Often conflicts between spouses reflect this struggle. But when Christ truly controls our lives and marriage, the power of the Holy Spirit enables us to resolve our differences and live in harmony. Christ does not war against Himself. If He is Lord of your life and that of your spouse, you will always experience His peace.

That's why we believe the Throne Check is absolutely necessary to a happy marriage. We encourage you to apply it regularly. You will discover, as we have, that growing together spiritually will give you the deepest intimacy you can experience.

The lessons we have shared with you in this book were not learned quickly; they were hammered out on the anvil of almost fifty years of experience in marriage. We believe that the basic principles we have discovered during our many years of marriage can, under the guidance and enabling of the Holy Spirit, help you build a vital, godly home despite the pressures that threaten to pull it apart.

> *These principles can help you build a vital, godly home despite the pressures that threaten to pull it apart.*

Being filled with the Spirit and using the Throne Check are practical ways in which you can meet the pressures of today and of the future. Another practical way to prepare for future service to your Lord is to develop a contract that expresses your commitment to our Lord and to each other, as described in Chapter 2.

These principles are not just words; they really work in building a lasting, harmonious relationship with two people who are committed to live together until "death do us part."

Vonette and I encourage you to use the four steps we have shared in this book to deepen your relationship. To summarize, these steps were:

1. *Enter into a partnership* with your spouse to provide a secure foundation to handle change and pressure.

2. *Establish God-centered priorities* to give your relationship direction and control through the storms of life.

3. *Develop "other-centeredness"* through praise, communication, and a healthy sex life to achieve greater wholeness and intimacy in your relationship.

4. *Build a godly home for your family.* Accept your children as God's plan for your childrearing years to ease the tension of parenting.

By following these steps, you will experience the immeasurable joy and richness of a marriage dedicated to the Lord and to each other. With God at the helm, you will know the satisfaction of a fulfilling, vibrant, fruitful relationship that comes from growing through the stresses in marriage.

A Spirit-Filled Calling

As you maintain your first love for Christ and invite the Holy Spirit to control and empower you, you can meet the many demands you face daily, and you will be establishing a strong basis from which to reach out to others.

God promises us victory, and most assuredly a life of genuine significance and personal fulfillment, as we respond to His call to help fulfill the Great Commission in our generation.

There's a world to be reached for Jesus Christ. The biblical values that have governed our society for the past two hundred years, particularly in the United States, are eroding rapidly. The world really is pulling apart, and godly homes are becoming more rare all the time. The Christian lifestyle is being viewed increasingly as outmoded. The biblical worldview is not understood, even in many so-called Christian homes. But God is calling individuals and couples to a radical commitment to make themselves available to share His love and forgiveness in the most positive and effective manner.

The last nearly fifty years have been an exciting adventure as we have chosen to obey God's call upon our lives. As a result, we have experienced and continue to experience the reality of God's promise in Ephesians 3:20: "Glory be to God who by his mighty power at work within us is able to do far more than we would ever dare to ask or even dream of—infinitely beyond our highest prayers, desires, thoughts, or hopes" (TLB). The blessings of God on our lives, our marriage, and our family have far exceeded our greatest expectations.

The world is waiting for the impact of your life. We invite you to come with us and help change our world.

Appendix

Preparing for the Golden Years

❧

By reaffirming their partnership, spouses can adapt to the changes of the empty nest and prepare for exciting, fruitful opportunities in their retirement.

The Empty Nest

VONETTE AND I were helping our youngest son, Brad, pack his car. He was leaving home—moving across the country to Washington, D.C., to work for Senator William Armstrong from Colorado.

Just before he left, the three of us got down on our knees in the living room to pray. When we rose, he embraced each of us. My eyes misted as I silently thanked God for such a wonderful son.

As we walked outside, my mind wandered back to the first day I left him at boarding school...

First we had helped Zac, by this time a seasoned college student, settle into his dorm room at Life Bible College in Los Angeles. Then, a few days later, I flew with sixteen-year-old Brad to Stoneybrook, a Christian preparatory school in New York, where through the generosity of dear friends he was given a scholarship.

When the two of us arrived, we lugged his bags to his room. Later, I met the faculty and spoke at chapel.

When the time came for me to go, I could see that Brad was anxious to get settled and meet the rest of the boys. I felt unneeded. And lonely.

The thought of saying goodbye made my throat tighten. A flood of tears threatened to spill down my face. Wiping away the dampness, I hurriedly prepared to leave. I didn't want to embarrass him.

By the time I reached the car, my tears flowed in earnest, and in the privacy of the rental car I told the Lord how much I would miss him...

I felt the same ache in my throat now. As Brad drove away toward Washington, D.C., we waved valiantly. I forced a smile and choked back my tears. *My little boy isn't little any more*, I thought as his car disappeared around a bend. *He's on his own now.*

And so were we. Zac had already left our nest and was soon to begin a family of his own, but I missed him just as much when he left.

I treasure these heartwarming memories of Zac and Brad. We'll always love our sons, and look forward to spending time with them whenever possible. But they are independent now. They don't need us like they did when they were young.

The empty nest stage of life can be the most exciting and creative time for couples. With the stress of child rearing only a memory, their marital relationship can grow deeper and richer. Even so, spouses face new challenges—those special stresses of the golden years.

Preparing for the Golden Years

No matter how we approach life, we age. Feeling older, however, doesn't always match the number of years a person has lived.

The legendary baseball player Satchel Paige used to challenge, "How old would you be if you didn't know how old you was?" If we think we are ancient, we will be. But if we live creative and adventurous lives, we defy the stereotypes of old age.

How can we live a full life despite the pressures of aging? By preparing for the years ahead. And by utilizing the lessons we have learned from the stresses of our past.

This gives us a distinct advantage. Unlike a bride and groom setting out into the unfamiliar territory of marriage, we who reach the golden years have gained some wisdom from our many pressure-filled circumstances. We can use this wisdom to manage or reduce the stresses of our senior years, and thus enjoy happy, fruitful lives.

Stress of the Empty Nest

The "empty nest syndrome" is a recent phenomenon created by increasing life expectancy. Before the medical advances of the 20th century, parents often did not survive long after their children left home. Today, however, many spouses live thirty to fifty years after their children are grown.

The empty nest brings with it a special set of stressors that can destroy a relationship. Many divorces occur at this period in the marriage cycle. This is so tragic, for these are the years when partners need each other for encouragement, comfort, and care.

Let's look briefly ate three of the major "golden age" stressors.

First, *loneliness*. Without children in the home, a marital relationship undergoes radical change. Couples who have centered their lives around their children find the empty nest a particularly painful period of adjustment. Over the years, their marriage may have lost its vitality. They discover that their relationship is merely a hollow shell, with nothing between them to prevent the loneliness.

Second, *boredom*. During this period, many spouses realize that their mate will never change those irritating habits nor conquer his weaknesses.

With children out of the nest, parents are forced into relating to each other. Spouses see their partner without the covering of parenthood. The only person to talk to at the dinner table is their mate. No energetic teenager livens their long evenings at home together. As a result, they find themselves wallowing in boredom and depression, resenting their bleak future and nurturing bad attitudes.

Third, *painful midlife adjustments*. Expectations and roles during the empty nest period change radically.

With her children gone, the wife is now free to pursue her occupation or ministry full-time. She may enter the job force or a ministry area for the first time in many years, eager to attain the goals she has put off for so long.

At the same time, her husband has discovered his limitations in the work world. His career has become routine and dull. With his wife at work, he no longer feels the center of her attention. Her new excitement and awareness makes him realize how tired he is of the corporate rat-race. With occupational stress at a peak, he wants a change.

Thus emotional stability is threatened. With no children at home for companionship and nurturing, the empty nest couple must reorganize their pattern of home life.

Yet the empty nest can be the beginning of a richer, fuller life. Many couples find profound satisfaction during this period. If they planned ahead, they have more financial resources and fewer expenses. They have fewer demands on their schedules. They have more time together and can concentrate fully on each other's company.

I encourage you to consider this time of life a gift from God to help you deepen your love for each other.

Making the Transition Less Stressful

Vonette and I dedicated Zac and Brad to God before they were born. Our sons have belonged to Him all these years. We were just responsible to rear them in the love and fear of our Lord and to give them the best training we could.

Even so, that final break when they left our nest was hard to accept.

Perhaps you are about to enter this difficult period. Or you are already experiencing the empty nest. Let me share three important principles that will help make your transition to the empty nest less stressful.

First, *let go*. As our children grow into their teens and become mature adults, we must consciously give them back to God's care. Letting go is no easy task, as you may have discovered. Accepting the empty nest with a positive attitude in the power of the Holy Spirit helps to lessen the pain of separation.

As your nest empties, no doubt you will shed tears as did Vonette and I when we released Zac and Brad to independence. But as you let go, God can fill the void with exciting and fruitful new opportunities and relationships. We have found delight in pouring our lives into each other in order that we may be more effective in our ministry for our Lord. We have also found more time to invest in the lives of many other young men and women and other adults as well.

Second, *accept the change*. Sadly, many couples respond to the stress of an empty nest in the same negative way they learned to handle other critical situations. They try to keep the status quo.

We can, however, develop new strategies for adapting at any stage of life.

Instead of holding onto old patterns of living, embrace new ways of doing things. Cultivate an open, teachable spirit. Rebuild your empty home through the power of the Holy Spirit.

Recognize that both you and your partner have also changed over the years. Don't expect that "newlywed couple" to reemerge after the children leave. Rather, begin reorganizing your relationship on the basis of who you are now instead of what you were years ago.

Third, *adopt a positive attitude*. Attitude makes all the difference in how couples adjust to the empty nest.

Self-pity and inflexibility only lengthen and aggravate a difficult transition. But a positive outlook opens our hearts and minds to the Lord's healing and helps ease the pain.

Vonette and I keep a positive attitude by welcoming the years ahead. We started alone, and once again we are enjoying "just the two of us." Though we believe the greatest investment we've made through the years is in the rearing of our sons, these present years in many ways are our most productive. We believe the best years of our lives are before us.

We urge you to taste the same joy. Rejoice in the partner God gave you. Plan to reap the benefits of your fruitful, godly life. Appreciate your life as it is. Look for the many positive results of growing older together.

Developing a Fuller Life in the Empty Nest

Think of what's happening to older couples in our society. A greater number of wives are entering the job market at middle age, or even later. One mother-turned-grand-mother, for example, became a nurse, specializing in pediatrics. More husbands are turning to a second career. We know a successful businessman who became a classroom teacher at forty-three.

You too can make the empty nest period an exciting and creative adventure. Let me share several practical suggestions to help you.

First, *step into the future.* Using the empty nest as a stepping stone to the future prepares couples for many rewards later. Determine to live an active, purposeful life—as did a banker who entered seminary to prepare for ministry at age forty-seven; as did a friend who enrolled in graduate school to earn a degree in social work at age fifty-six.

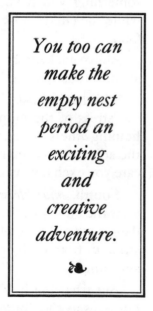

You too can make the empty nest period an exciting and creative adventure.

I encourage you to decide which direction the Lord would have you take when your parenting days are over. Then use your extra time, money, and concentration to set out on that path.

Second, *expand your horizons.* Living in an empty nest can be especially tedious if we have too narrow a focus. We must expand our horizons.

One way is to develop new ministries. One couple, for example, looked at their four-bedroom home and wondered what to do with all the space. Then they had an idea. Why not start weekend retreats?

Once a month, they invited ten people to their home on Friday evening through mid-day Saturday. They tried to include at least one person or couple who hadn't committed their lives to Jesus Christ. Guests could choose to sleep over or go back to their homes and return for breakfast. The group studied the Bible and prayed for each other during this time.

With a little imagination, you can think of other things to do. You could begin a ministry to international students. Or use your extra time for discipleship and evangelism. You may wish to travel to a part of the country you have never seen. Learn a new hobby or craft. Teach illiterate adults to read. Plant a garden. Whatever your activity, do something you have always wanted to do but couldn't while the children were at home, and do it for the glory of God.

Above all, keep growing. Use your creative abilities and adventurous spirit to improve your partnership.

Third, *enrich your friendships*. An effective way to reduce the stress of the empty nest is to dedicate your time to helping others. When you pour your life into someone else, the adjustments you make will be easier. The rapport and care you exchange with friends will soothe the lonely days.

Fourth, *enjoy life with your partner*. Now Vonette and I view the empty nest as a second honeymoon. Joyful, abundant partnership means receiving our major rewards and strength from each other. It requires sharing our interests and time.

But what fun it is! We laughingly refer to this time of our lives as the "brighter years." And we are looking forward to the rest of our lives with great anticipation.

Growing in Retirement

DWIGHT AND Audrey Swanson were returning from their first trip as a retired couple. Dwight had completed an active forty-year career in business, most recently as CEO for a large, profitable utilities company based in Des Moines. They decided that they were entitled to some leisure and time off. Then they wandered into a meeting held by Campus Crusade...

Ray and Burnette Whitehead's lives were full and productive. Ray was the founder and president of an engineering company. Burnette was involved in cultural and other activities with their children. At fifty-three, Ray decided to take an early retirement...

What do these couples have in common? Open to God's leading in their lives, they embarked on exciting new adventures during a time when other Christians are content to sit idle.

In recent years, Vonette and I have felt burdened for that strategic segment of society who possess a phenomenal, even revolutionary potential for serving God—those sixty years and older. We envision many older couples serving Christ together in ways they never dreamed possible. We see them growing and learning through their retirements years, and using their talents and skills until the end of their lives.

Preparing for Retirement

The stresses of the golden years defeat many Christian mates. Although we begin aging the moment we are born, often it isn't until our forties that we become aware of a gradual deterioration. As we move on in years, the rate of decline increases. No longer do experience and knowledge compensate for losses through aging. Couples we know who are in their young to middle years seem to look younger every year—a constant reminder that we have entered the last third of our lives.

Perhaps you are approaching retirement. What can you do to prepare for this stage of your life and reduce the stress of these twilight years? From our personal experiences, Vonette has these suggestions:

Vonette

First, *accept your age*. Did you know that Grandma Moses began oil painting at age seventy-five? And that she created her most famous work, *Christmas Eve*, at 101?

Or that Bach composed some of his best music at eighty-five? That Ronald Reagan became president of the United States, the most powerful and influential office in the secular world, at seventy and completed his second term of office at seventy-eight?

We could list many others who have made remarkable achievements in contributions to their fellow man in their golden years.

The Scriptures also record men and women who experienced and accomplished great things in their old age.

Sarah and Abraham started a family well beyond childrearing years. Joshua and Caleb led the Hebrew army across the Jordan to conquer the Promised Land when they were in their eighties.

The Lord regards the elderly with high honor (Leviticus 19:32). Rejoice that He has given you so many years. Thank Him for every moment, each ability, and all the relationships you enjoy.

Do as Solomon urged and "rejoice in the wife of your youth" (Proverbs 5:18, TLB). Be grateful for every day you spend with your partner.

Face the reality of your situation. Don't futilely search for ways to keep yourself eternally young. Accept your limitations.

If you experience pain or loss as part of your aging process, live graciously day by day through the power of the Holy Spirit.

Second, *make peace with life.* To make peace with life, we must accept the certainty of our own death and that of our partner. When we realize that change is a part of God's loving plan for us, we can prepare for the sorrows we inevitably encounter. Put your mate's health and life in His hands. Ask God to strengthen your courage and bolster your hope, even as illness and death take their toll.

We have discovered that by flowing with the ups and downs of life in the power of the Holy Spirit, we can use the circumstances and stresses of the golden years to grow as a couple and to deepen our spiritual walk with the Lord.

Third, *retrain for a career with fewer physical demands.* Perhaps like us, you may not want to retire. You may wish to continue your present ministry or career long after most people have opted for the Gold Watch, Social Security, and a rocking chair.

But what if you have no choice? What happens when your employer decides that it's time for you to move on?

Even if you can continue your career, will you be physically up to it? Are you preparing for that event?

Choosing and training now for a career that you can handle in retirement is a wise decision if you plan to continue in the work force.

Fourth, *prepare for a loss of income.* Many senior citizens cannot maintain the salary or wages they earned in their fifties or early sixties. Retirement may mean going from two paychecks to none. You may find your resources stretched to the limit. What can you do to ease this problem? Here are a few ideas:

- Start a retirement fund early in your career.
- Set a budget before you quit work.
- Take care of major expenditures ahead of time, like replacing worn appliances or reroofing your home.
- Reduce your debt.
- Keep saving and investing after you retire to help curb spending and slow the depletion of your reserve.
- Obtain counsel from a godly, competent financial advisor.

God controls events. No matter how much we plan, we have no assurance of a quiet, secure tomorrow. But our dependence on the Lord instead of our preparations will enable us to live fruitful, abundant lives through all of our circumstances.

Fifth, *keep active.* Our culture offers two views on aging.

One says that retirees should gradually pull away from former pursuits. Peace and contentment come only by withdrawing from an active role in society.

The other view holds that senior citizens must remain active at all costs. The elderly are not much different from middle-aged adults. Except for slowing down somewhat, older persons should work and participate in other activities as they once did.

Both views are valid when kept in balance. As we age, we will be progressively more limited in what we can do. Yet, if we listen and respond to God's voice, He will enable us to minister actively to the end of our lives.

Living a Productive Life

Have you ever heard older Christians remark, "I've served the Lord for many years. Now it's time for me to sit back and let the younger people take over"?

God may change our ministry as we grow older, but He never asks us to retire from His work. At every age, we must be open to His calling.

Mrs. Erma Griswold, Bill's valued associate for more than twenty-five years, joined Campus Crusade at a time when most people stop working. But at sixty-seven, she was just getting started.

As a volunteer to our ministry, she had a worldwide influence. She lightened Bill's load tremendously and inspired all of our office staff by her faithful service.

At ninety-three she was a godly example of how productive the golden years can be.

Dwight and Audrey Swanson are another example. Bill relates the story:

Bill

They had just taken their first trip as retirees. To end the month-long vacation, they stopped in Hershey, Pennsylvania, where Dwight had a speaking engagement at a utilities stockholders meeting.

While walking through the hotel, they discovered a musical group rehearsing for a Campus Crusade seminar and dinner that evening.

Since they had contributed to the ministry in the past, Dwight and Audrey decided to attend the seminar after he addressed the stockholders. At the end of the Campus Crusade meeting, they joined a reception line to greet us.

As we talked, I learned that Dwight had just retired from forty years in business.

"God sent you!" I exclaimed. "I've been praying for retired businessmen to provide our ministry with professional administrative help."

Although Dwight wasn't looking forward to assuming weighty responsibilities, he and Audrey visited Arrowhead Springs, where a short time later they decided to join this ministry.

For the first year, Dwight held the position of administrative associate. Then he became vice president of administration. His expertise in organizing people was invaluable.

Audrey joined the Campus Crusade Wives' Advisory Board. She worked with the Clothes Closet, a program to help fill the needs of Crusade staff facing a financial crisis or returning from overseas missions. She also became a prayer coordinator for Associates in Media, a Campus Crusade ministry in Hollywood.

Because of their availability, Dwight and Audrey gave productive service beyond retirement, and their time with Campus Crusade was rewarding and fruitful.

God may not ask you to move across the country to be a full-time volunteer in a Christian organization like Campus Crusade, but if you are available He will reveal ways in which you can be fruitful for Him where you are. Keep yourself open to the Holy Spirit's leading, and He will direct you to a fulfilling ministry.

I cannot think of a more rewarding ministry than being an intercessor. As you have more free time, spend it in the Lord's presence. Pray for your loved ones and friends who have not yet received Christ as their Savior and Lord. Intercede for your neighbors, your church, your pastor, a missionary. Lift up our leaders in government. Claim 2 Chronicles 7:14 for our nation. Pray for a revival to come to our beloved land and a worldwide spiritual harvest.

I encourage you to use your creative abilities and talents to reach others for Christ.

I also encourage you to use your creative abilities and talents to reach others for Christ. If there are children in your neighborhood, adopt a "grandchild," loving and introducing him to God's love and forgiveness through Jesus Christ. Or join the visitation team at your church.

Use your hobby as an opportunity to share Christ. While teaching a knitting class or delivering homemade meals to invalids, share your testimony of how God has given you new life through Jesus Christ.

Live simply. Lay up your treasures in heaven. Don't invest all of your resources in things of this world. When the Lord Jesus Christ makes you aware of the needs of others, be ready to help them. There is a law of God: What you sow, you will reap (Galatians 6:7). The more you help others, the more God will bless and help you.

I urge you to step out in faith into new areas of Christian service. Don't let opportunities to share Christ and minister to others in His name slip by during your golden years.

Enjoying life is another secret to a productive retirement. If you start planning projects or volunteer work that excites you before you retire, the transition can be uplifting rather than depressing.

In addition to using your creative abilities and investing yourself in others, consider the little ways you could make your life happier after you quit work. Sleep in a little later in the morning. Walk. Read those books you have put off so long. Beautify your garden. Take time to enjoy God's marvelous creation. Find exciting things to do with your mate.

We have discovered that one of the greatest enjoyments a couple can have during their golden years is grandparenting. We love to play with our grandchildren, take them places, tell them stories from our past, and listen to their chatter.

The Fullness of the Golden Years

A wise counselor once told Job, "You shall live a long, good life; like standing grain, you'll not be harvested until it's time!" (Job 5:26, TLB).

Ray and Burnette Whitehead are examples of this.

An early retirement was anything but the beginning of a quiet life for them. When Ray left his contracting business at fifty-three to join our ministry, the busiest part of his life began.

Those years took them to two other continents to live. For a year Ray put his business skills to work at our Arrowhead Springs headquarters, engineering and excavating for the village conference center, amphitheater, and office complex.

For six years, they lived in Latin America. Much of their time there was spent organizing evangelistic breakfasts and dinners for government and business leaders and their wives.

When they moved back to the United States, they ministered to executives, helping them see how they could invest in God's work around the world. When our South African staff decided to start a similar ministry, Ray and Burnette took a group of executives from the United States to participate in South Africa's first Executive Seminar.

After leading a few more tours to Africa, this dedicated couple decided to move there. Their primary aim was to minister to the leaders of South Africa's Black Homelands. With three special assets—his white hair, his nationality, and his boldness—Ray befriended and ministered to many who had not been reached for Christ.

"As long as I'm physically able," Ray affirmed, "I'll never be satisfied unless I'm right in the thick of the battle. I could have made a lot of money if I'd kept working. But if God can use me to see one soul turn to Him, it's worth all that. We don't have a lot of money, but we've never lived so well—or been so happy and content."[1]

---

[1] Lee Gilliland, "Whitehead Talks, Africans Listen," *Worldwide Challenge* (February 1982), pp. 40–42.

How about you? Are you experiencing what they have discovered? That the later years truly are golden as ripened grain? We urge you to dedicate your entire life and marriage to the service of our gracious Savior, Jesus Christ.

Practical Resources for Strengthening Your Home

Transferable Concepts. Bill Bright. These concepts offer principles that lead to a happier marriage. Available in booklet, video, and audio.

How You Can Experience God's Love and Forgiveness

How You Can Be Filled With the Holy Spirit

How You Can Walk in the Spirit

How You Can Love By Faith

How You Can Experience the Adventure of Giving

HomeBuilders—Small-Group Studies for Couples. Various authors. Series includes such topics as *Managing Pressure in Your Marriage* by Dennis Rainey and Robert Lewis, *Life Choices for a Lasting Marriage* by David Boehi, *Mastering Your Money in Marriage* by Ron Blue, *Building Your Marriage* by Dennis Rainey, and others. HomeBuilders Church Starter Kit and Leader's Kit also available.

Building Your Mate's Self-Esteem. Dennis and Barbara Rainey. This practical book helps you tap into God's formula for building up your mate. Find out how to overcome problems from your past, your peers, and your parents. Learn how to help your mate conquer self-doubt, how to improve communication, and much more.

Loving Your Marriage Enough to Protect It. Jerry B. Jenkins. In a candid style, the author shares ways you can protect your marriage against marital infidelity and a lifetime of regret.

The New Dare to Discipline. Dr. James Dobson. Here is a completely revised and expanded work from Dr. Dobson's earlier book. More than mere advice about raising children, this book provides a game plan to help parents understand their kids and handle everyday challenges as they arise.

Have You Made the Wonderful Discovery of the Spirit-Filled Life? Bill Bright. Discover the reality of the Spirit-filled life and how to live in moment-by-moment dependence on Him.

The Holy Spirit: The Key to Supernatural Living. Bill Bright. This book helps you enter into the Spirit-filled life and shares how you can experience a life of supernatural power and victory.

Keys to Dynamic Living card. Bill Bright. Experience a joyful, fruitful, Spirit-filled life and deal with temptation through "Spiritual Breathing." Small enough to tuck into your pocket, purse, or Bible.

Available through your local Christian bookstore, mail-order catalog distributor, or NewLife Publications.